DEALS . . .
DEALS . . .
AND MORE
DEALS

DEALS . . .
DEALS . . .
AND MORE
DEALS

Risk Arbitrage –

The Announcement of a Merger is the Beginning of an Opportunity

Second Edition
by
Regina M. Pitaro

Gabelli University Press
New York

Library of Congress Cataloging in Publication Data
Pitaro, Regina M.

Deals . . . Deals . . . And More Deals
0-9678320-0-4

This publication is intended to provide guidance in regard to the subject matter covered. It is sold with the understanding that the author and publisher are not herein engaged in rendering legal, accounting, tax or other professional services. If such services are required, professional assistance should be sought.

Printed in the United States of America

Acknowledgments

This book is the culmination of many years of work by several professionals in the world of arbitrage.

The idea to create a book on arbitrage investing first came from Mario Gabelli, to whom I owe a huge thank you. While Mario's reputation as a stellar value investor is legendary on Wall Street, many people do not know that he is also a world class arbitrageur. His brilliance, inspiration, creative ideas and boundless energy are responsible for this book's existence.

Eugene Bernardin and Raffaele Rocco, my friends and colleagues, worked tirelessly to retrieve information about specific deals and lent their expertise to every aspect of the investment process. I owe them a huge debt of gratitude for their time and dedication.

A very special thank you to Paolo Vicinelli, my co-author, without whose arbitrage expertise, hard work, and great patience this project would not have been possible.

Thank you to Randy Heck, for his work on so many deals; to Lisa Salibello, for her unconditional support and marketing savvy; and Maureen Naccari, for her creative talent in designing this book.

Contents

Proxy Solicitors
The Press
The Intermediaries
The Regulators
The Target Company and the Board

Bear Hugs
The American Bear Hug: Home Products and Cyanamid
Proxy Battles
IBM Goes Hostile
Hostile Tenders – The "Grizzly Bear"

Anticipatory Defenses
Poison Pill
Staggered Board
Other Shark Repellents
Pennzoil Fights off UPR – Just Say No
Post-Bid Defenses
Standstill Agreement
Pac Man Defense
Greenmail
Selling the Crown Jewel
Self-Tender
White Nights
Hilton and ITT – The White Night

Methods of Valuation
EBITDA
Earnings Per Share
Assets
Gabelli Asset Management
LIN Television Corporation
Hudson General

This announcement appears as a matter of record only.

GABELLI ARBITRAGE FUND

A private arbitrage partnership organized under the laws of the State of New York.

$9,175,000

The undersigned arranged the private placement of these securities

———————

GABELLI & COMPANY, INC.

January 31. 1985

Chapter 1: The Eighth Wonder of the World

The Rice Parable

There was once a king who lived in a far away land. In order to repay the local sage for saving the life of his daughter, the king offered to give the sage anything he wanted. But the humble wise man first refused to accept a reward for his service to the king. Upon the king's insistence, the wise man finally agreed to what seemed to be a modest payment. He asked for one grain of rice – the amount to be doubled each day. The sage would receive one grain of rice that day, two the next day, four the next, and so on. The king agreed to it, thinking nothing of giving away a few grains of rice on a daily basis.

But it was only a matter of weeks before the king's granaries were empty and the sage had become the richest man in the land. In fact, after only one month, the king was paying the sage over 1 billion grains of rice a day. How did one grow to over one billion in just 31 days? The power of compounding – a true wonder. In no style of investment is the magic of compounding more evident than risk arbitrage. This book will unveil the mystery of arbitrage - not as a black magic art, but rather as an essential component in an investor's portfolio.

Risk Arbitrage

In Berkshire Hathaway's 1988 letter to shareholders, Warren Buffett reworded an old Wall Street proverb into: "Give a man a fish and you feed him for a day. Teach him how to arbitrage and you feed him forever." He was referring to the power of consistent, predictable returns from an investment methodology about which most of the investing public knows very little: arbitrage.

Arbitrage, as defined in most dictionaries, is the process by which you profit from price differences when the same security, commodity, or currency is traded on two or more markets. The astute arbitrageur will buy the security in the market where it is trading at a low price and sell that same security in the market where it trades at a higher price, netting the difference.

Savvy traders have used arbitrage since the day some cave dweller noticed that saber-toothed tiger hides brought higher prices on glacial plains than in the jungle. (The saber-toothed tiger being a much rarer commodity on a glacier than in a jungle). He would get a contract to sell hides in the north and buy in the south, locking in a profitable spread. After expenses, of course.

In a more modern setting, an arbitrageur might simultaneously buy a gold contract on the London Metals Exchange and sell a contract for a like amount of gold in the Chicago market, locking in a profit because gold is priced higher in Chicago than in London. An equity arbitrageur might buy shares of IBM in London at $120 per share and simultaneously sell those shares in New York, where they are trading at $120½, a premium to the price in London. These are two of the many forms that arbitrage takes.

Today's most prevalent form of arbitrage is merger arbitrage, or what is commonly referred to in the trade as risk arbitrage. Risk arb is the simple bet that an announced merger will definitely be completed. In making such a bet, an arbitrageur purchases the stock of a company that is going to be acquired by another corporation, but is trading in the market at a price that is lower than its deal price. When the deal closes, the risk arbitrageur has netted a profit on the difference between the price at which he bought his stock and the price that is paid for that stock by the acquiring company. By investing in such secure and stable announced merger transactions, arbitrageurs can earn a consistent and attractive absolute rate of return with very low risk.

The Power of Compounding

There are many advantages to investing in risk arbitrage. Let's focus on three: risk arbitrage returns are not closely correlated with those of the stock market; they are less volatile than returns on the S&P 500; and longer term they are higher than those returns afforded by traditional investing. While these three factors provide for excellent results in the world of arbitrage, the real beauty of risk arb investing is that there is rarely a down year. Because risk arb returns are consistently positive year in and year out, they fulfill the concept of a compound return. We proclaim this source of compounded earnings as the eighth wonder of the world.

Compounding is the secret to wealth creation over a period of decades. If your principal compounds annually with rarely a down year, you will accumulate impressive growth in invested capital over the longer term. Conversely, if your returns are substantial, but are broken every few years by a down market, they will suffer a great deal. The secret to prevent this from happening is to never break the chain of up years. Don't break the chain.

Take the example of the island of Manhattan. In 1624, the Dutch paid just $24 in beads to purchase the island of Manhattan. A purchase of Manhattan today, in 1999, would run you approximately 10 trillion dollars – that is $10,000,000,000,000. That $10 trillion would buy you substantially all of the real estate on the island today. Any reasonable person would look at this investment made by the Dutch and marvel at the return they would have today, growing $24 into $10 trillion, had they held onto their purchase for the last 375 years.

As miraculous as the return appears to be, the exact same return could have been earned in an even simpler fashion. If the Dutch had invested their $24 over the same period in any security that yielded just 7.4% annually, their money would also be worth $10 trillion today. That is, the amazing return that was earned on the island of Manhattan was equal to an annually compounded return of just 7.4%. The trick to this compounding is that there could not have been a down year. A break in the chain would have altered profits. Many breaks in the chain would have substantially lowered the buildup in net worth.

A quick example of two investors should finalize this compounding argument. Assume that Alice and Bob both invest $1 million of their 401(k) accounts in the year 2000. Alice puts her money into a risk arbitrage fund that ends up returning 12% each year for the next ten years. By the power of compounding, she has tripled her money to $3.1 million by the year 2010. Bob, on the other hand, puts his money into an aggressive fund that offers substantial upside, albeit with a higher degree of risk. The fund in which he invests ends up with gains of 20% in eight of the ten years, but is *down* 20% in year 1 and year 6. By the year 2010, Bob has $2.7 million compared to Alice's $3.1 million. Even though Bob's returns were almost 2 times Alice's returns in eight of the ten years, his final accumulation of wealth was less. This was because his chain of compounding was interrupted every five years.

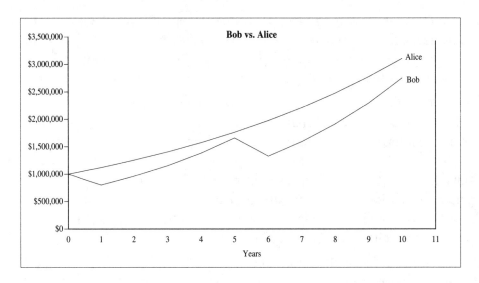

The Magic of Arbitrage – Don't Break the Chain

One of the quintessential ways to reap the benefits of the compounding effect is to invest one's assets in a risk arbitrage fund. More later.

The practice of merger arbitrage has arisen from the numerous takeovers and consolidations that have transformed business in the past forty years. Since World War II, we have seen three major waves of merger and acquisition activity. Each wave has been substantially greater than the last and they are discussed in detail in Chapter 3. We are currently in the midst of the 1990s merger wave – the largest that business has ever seen. In 1998, there were 7800 mergers in the U.S. alone accounting for $1.6 trillion in merger and acquisition (M&A) activity. This has created nirvana for the arbitrageurs investing in these deals and considerable wealth for the investors in risk arbitrage funds.

The Deal

In the world of arbitrage, the cycle begins with the announcement of a merger proposal or hostile offer. When a deal event happens, there is a buyer and a seller. In the simplest form of such a transaction, the buyer makes an offer for the seller's stock, almost always at a premium to the market price of the seller's stock. While the stock of the selling company trades higher on the announcement of the deal, it generally stays below the deal price until the merger is completed.

Consider when Johnson & Johnson offered to buy Neutrogena in 1994 for $35.25 a share. After the announcement of the deal, Neutrogena traded at $34.75 in the open market. This was up from $22 a share before speculation that a deal was in the works had taken Neutrogena stock higher. Any retail investor, and most institutional investors, very likely sold their stock at $34.75, giving up the remaining $0.50 potential upside if the deal were completed, to avoid the potential $13 downside should the deal fall apart and Neutrogena go back to $22. Because of price risk, the stock remained below the deal price of $35.25 and created opportunity for the arbitrageurs. The arbs came in and bought Neutrogena stock, profiting from the $0.50 spread between the deal and market prices.

Given the above example, an investor may question the safety of such investing -- $0.50 upside, $13 downside. The key is that if an arbitrage fund's assets are invested across a spectrum of many such announced deals, it is unlikely that even the collapse of one or two deals in a year will substantially crimp overall portfolio returns. Because there is such downside risk in each deal, diversification across many deals is extremely important. As long as the arbitrage portfolio is diversified, it improves the likelihood that returns will accrue gradually, in a much less volatile manner than in a traditional stock-picking fund.

Furthermore, the returns earned on risk arbitrage funds are generally not correlated to the market. For those who categorize investment approaches, risk arb falls under the category of event-driven investing. What a risk arb fund returns in any given year is generally not tied to the return of the S&P 500 or Dow Jones Industrial Average. Because of its consistent, profitable returns that are uncorrelated with the market, a risk arb fund behaves similarly to an optimally well diversified portfolio. As such, steady profits are accrued in almost any market environment.

This Book

The myriad of deals announced annually will continue to provide today's arbitrageurs with plentiful opportunity and rewarding profits. Therefore, informed investors can decide for themselves whether arbitrage fills a role in their portfolio structure.

The goal of this book is to explain arbitrage and the role of the arbitrageur in today's markets. This will be done largely through the analysis of deals in which the Gabelli arbitrage portfolio team has invested over the past twenty years.

In the next two chapters, the history of risk arbitrage will be explained. We trace the roots of arbitrage from medieval times up through the turn of the century merger movement in 1900 and on through the M&A developments of the 1960s, 80s, and 90s. We explain what has driven each of these merger waves and how they have consistently provided the arbitrageurs with profitable returns.

Once the historic framework is in place, readers will uncover how merger arbitrage works today. The core issue of risk versus return is laid out in Chapter 4. This chapter uncovers the basis of risk arbitrage and the various deal components that an arb analyst evaluates before making his investment decision. The analysis is then put to work in Chapter 5, as we walk the reader through a standard deal from the eyes of an arbitrageur. Applying the fundamentals of arbitrage analysis, we show how to evaluate an investment in the aforementioned Johnson & Johnson – Neutrogena deal.

Chapters 6 and 7 go on to discuss the various types of deals that are available for the arbitrageur to invest in. These deals range from the standard cash tender offer to more complex transactions involving stubs and recapitalizations. For each deal, we give a real life example of an arbitrage investment in that particular type of transaction.

In Chapter 8 we overview the roles of various participants involved in merger activity. We explain why it is important for an arbitrageur to know the role of each party involved and how each can affect the eventual outcome of a merger deal.

Chapters 9 and 10 get into the battlefield tactics that are employed in hostile transactions. Chapter 9 details approaches that different hostile acquirers use in various circumstances. We explain why the arbitrageur has to be familiar with the weapons at the disposal of the hostile buyer and how these can ensure the completion of a deal. In Chapter 10, we turn to the defense mechanisms that are used by tenacious managers who want to keep their companies independent. Understanding how these defenses work, and more importantly whether or not they will work, can mean the difference between big arbitrage profits and staggering losses from a failed takeover attempt.

In the final chapter of the book, we discuss the role of fundamental analysis in arbitrage situations and how it is integrated into the overall investment approach at Gabelli Asset Management. Although risk arbitrage is an event-driven style of investment, fundamental research plays an important role. This will be made clear through the analysis of two mergers, LIN Television and Hudson General.

All combined, these chapters run through the check list that a risk arbitrageur considers in his investment analysis. While we may not make you a world-class arbitrageur, we will unveil the art behind risk arbitrage investing. Once you understand the basics behind the art form of arbitrage and the returns that it consistently yields on an annual basis, there should be little question in your mind that risk arbitrage is the eighth wonder of the world.

◆ ◆ ◆

Chapter 2: Early History of Arbitrage

The term 'risk arbitrage' evokes connotations of a modern day trading desk where Wall Street analysts, seeking to invest in mergers, scrutinize complex transactions. While this may be true today, arbitrage activity has a long and storied history. In fact, the roots of arbitrage can be traced as far back as medieval times.

In the Medieval period, Venetian merchants used several different forms of currency to pay for goods and services. Currencies ranged from valuable coins to precious metals to the actual money that was used at the time. Because there was no set value for any of these, astute merchants would often trade one currency for another, benefiting from someone else's misperception of the value of their currency. The merchants profited from the price differentials that existed between these seemingly identical commodities. In a very crude sense of the word, this was arbitrage.

In another form of early, rudimentary arbitrage, the London merchant bank of Rothschild was able to profit from Wellington's victory over Napoleon at the Battle of Waterloo in 1815. When carrier pigeons sent Rothschild advance news of Napoleon's defeat, Rothschild used the information of the British victory to reap big gains via the purchase of British Government Bonds. Rothschild had taken advantage of a security that traded lower in a certain market (London) because the flow of information had kept the true value of the security from being factored into its price.

In the United States, the history of risk arbitrage can be traced back to the great consolidators of the 1800s and the merger boom that took place at the end of that century. The latter half of the 1800s saw the amassing of great fortunes by the famed financiers of that time: Rockefeller, Carnegie, Morgan, and Vanderbilt. These business titans were the founders of the largest corporations of their period, many of which still exist today. They built their companies through mergers with competitors, spurring the nation's first real wave of deal activity. Needless to say, this gave rise to the practice known today as merger arbitrage. Because mergers and acquisitions are the basis upon which risk arbitrage is performed, it is important to to reflect on the history of merger activity in the United States.

Restructuring the Railroads

In the nineteenth century, the railroad industry dominated business. It consumed the nation's finances, with as much capital invested into it as all other industries combined. Sixty percent of the companies listed on the New York Stock Exchange were railroad firms. As could be expected, the railroad boom attracted all types of investors, from the prominent Cornelius Vanderbilt to the corrupt and disreputable predators present in most investment manias. But by 1890, many railroads had been overbuilt and were highly leveraged. So, when the great economic depression of 1893-1897 hit, many of the rail companies were unable to service their debt payments. The depression resulted in the bankruptcy of 169 rail companies, close to 25% of the industry.

Just as the rail industry appeared to be collapsing in turmoil, James Pierpont Morgan stepped into the fray. In the late nineteenth century, Morgan had made a name for himself as an incredibly savvy investment banker. By the mid-1890s, many of his clients had significant holdings in the railroad industry and this spurred Morgan to act. It resulted in the consolidation of hundreds of railroad firms and the shutting down of overlapping lines. This consolidation in the rail industry would set the tone for mergers and acquisitions for much of the twentieth century.

Morgan's primary role in the restructuring process was the recapitalization of the rail firms. In this process, his bank restructured the firm's debt and issued new securities that would be exchanged for the old debt when the rail company emerged from bankruptcy. These new securities were highly speculative and began trading on a 'when-issued' basis (a when-issued security is one that has been authorized and trades in the market but has not yet been officially issued). They also traded at a premium to the old, underlying debt. This created an arbitrage opportunity because the underlying and the when-issued were, in essence, the same security, but traded at different prices.

The arbitrage community began selling short the when-issued securities and buying the cheaper underlying debt. When the rails emerged from bankruptcy, the long and short holdings of the arb would cancel out. In essence, his position would disappear. The arb's profit came on the price difference between what he had paid for the cheaper underlying debt, and for what he had sold the more expensive when-issued security. Regardless of whether the price of the security went up or down, the arbitrageur realized a gain on the spread that he had locked in. In this manner, the restructuring of the railroads gave birth to risk arbitrage, as we know it today.

The Turn of the Century Merger Movement - Railroads, Oil, and Steel

The peak of this dynamic merger wave came between 1898 and 1902. In that time, over 2600 merger-related transactions took place in the manufacturing sector, with a total value of approximately $6.3 billion. This would equate to almost $120 billion in 1999. There was ample opportunity for arbitrageurs and ample reasons for the consolidation.

Three primary reasons existed for the merger boom at the turn of the century. First, the industrial revolution had spurred rapid growth in the manufacturing sector, resulting in many small but disorganized producers across industries. It was simply more efficient for these companies to join together and realize economies of scale and pricing power. Second, for the first time in the history of the United States, capital had become readily available through the likes of J.P. Morgan. Finally, the regulatory environment in the U.S. was conducive to mergers. While the Sherman-Anti Trust Act of 1890 came down hard on price fixing through cartels, it allowed mergers between competing firms.

Apart from the railroads, other industrial companies were beginning to develop in the latter half of the nineteenth century. Many of these firms were small, one-plant operations that created an overcrowded industrial landscape. In the oil business, John D. Rockefeller set out to terminate the relentless competition that existed. Beginning with an investment in a small Cleveland refinery, Rockefeller pursued a strategy of vertical integration and acquisition in which he assumed control of one oil company after another. By 1880, he had created an industrial empire that controlled over 90 percent of the nation's oil production. In 1882, he formally organized the Standard Oil Trust, in which individual refiners exchanged their own shares in return for new trust certificates. As all major oil producers joined into the trust, the tone was set for the wave of mergers and arbitrage opportunity that was about to occur across all industrial businesses.

The signature deal of this period was the formation of United States Steel in 1901. In a manner similar to that employed by Rockefeller in the oil industry, Andrew Carnegie amassed a fortune in the U.S. steel business. At the turn of the century, Carnegie Steel was one of the few large industrial companies in the United States. In late 1900, the president of Carnegie Steel convinced J.P. Morgan that a consolidation of all of the nation's leading steel companies would produce tremendous synergies and cost savings. Morgan agreed and quickly organized an underwriting syndicate that would finance the merger of Carnegie Steel and nine other steel industry companies into the first-ever billion dollar company: U.S. Steel.

Morgan's role in the deal was to organize the financing and to serve as the leader of the group that put it all together. In this capacity, he had to regulate the exchange of the new securities for those companies coming into the deal. He had to offer those shareholders assurance of a minimum market value for their stock and some amount of liquidity for the holders that wanted cash. This created an arbitrage opportunity that was not much different from the merger arbitrage that many funds do today. Confident of the receipt of a certain value for the stocks of the firms being rolled in to U.S. Steel, arbitrageurs could buy these stocks on the open market and expect to profit when the deal was consummated. The formation of U.S. Steel was soon completed with the value of the transaction at $1.4 billion. Adjusted for inflation this would stand as the largest merger ever until Kohlberg, Kravis, Roberts' 1989 buyout of RJR-Nabisco.

The Regulators Strike Back - Trustbusters

All great things must come to an end and the merger boom at the turn of the century did just that. While it may have been a 'great thing' for the Morgans, and the Rockefellers of the nation, critics complained that the mergers had left industrial power in the hands of too few corporations. They claimed that the lack of competition left the consumer vulnerable to price fixing. The critics had a reasonable argument. The merger frenzy resulted in companies like International Harvester cornering an 85% share of the farm equipment market and the American Tobacco Company capturing 80% of the nation's tobacco business.

The administration of President William Taft (also known as 'The Trustbuster') went after the newly formed conglomerates in an effort to undo the activities of the past twenty years. The legislation that ensued set the groundwork for 20th century mergers and still largely regulates arbitrage activity today. In 1911, the Supreme Court forced the breakup of Standard Oil. Reflecting the public opinion of that time, the court ruled that such monopolistic power was against the laws of the country. Three years later, Congress passed the Clayton Antitrust Act of 1914. The Clayton Act was an amendment to clarify and supplement the Sherman Antitrust Act, which had been ineffective in its prevention of industry consolidation. The act prohibited intercorporate stock holdings and interlocking directorates in corporations capitalized at $1 million or more in the same field of business. One year later, in 1915, the Federal Trade Commission (FTC) was established. Its responsibility was to promote free and fair competition through the enforcement of certain antitrust laws.

The breakup of 'big business' would be one of the single most important events in arbitrage in the twentieth century. Standard Oil represented the first breakup of a company against the will of its management and shareholders. For the arbitrageur, a bet that a deal would be consummated was no longer a sure one. From this point on, regulators like the FTC would closely scrutinize all merger transactions.

The Roaring Twenties

The end of World War I, in 1918, was followed by a brief period of postwar recession. The recession began in early 1920 and lasted for only about a year and a half. But this, of course, is not the matter for which the 1920s are remembered. Rather, the 1920s in the United States are best recalled as a period of giddy enthusiasm, grand entertainment, and a confidence in America's economic future that fueled the stock market to unprecedented levels. During this time, the United States became the world's leading economic and financial power. The Dow Jones Industrial Average soared from a post-war low of 70 to its August 1929 peak of 381, a 443% return in less than a decade. Along with all of this enthusiasm came another wave of mergers.

The 1920s merger movement was fueled by a rising stock market and renewed industrial growth. While established industries like oil, steel, and utilities continued to expand, new sectors like airplanes and automobiles began to flourish. Risk arbitrage was still in its infancy, but tremendous merger activity spurred its growth. Between 1926 and 1930, close to 1000 companies a year were gobbled up by other corporations. During this time, over 4600 mergers were announced.

The buyout boom of the 1920s began when Henry Ford did a leveraged buyout of the minority shareholders in his Ford Motor Company. In 1919, he paid $105.8 million to acquire the 41% of the company that he did not already own. The price he paid valued the company at 3.4 times its 1919 earnings of $75 million. Just a few years later, Ford would turn down an offer of $1 billion for the whole firm.

The Ford buyout was similar to many of today's transactions that are extremely profitable to the arbitrageur. His initial bid of $7,500 a share was eventually raised to $12,500 a share. Any arbitrageur who had bought Ford stock on the original $7,500 announcement would have realized tremendous profits when the minority stake was eventually sold for $12,500 a share.[1]

The 1920s merger wave would last until October of 1929, at which time the Dow Jones Industrial Average plummeted 40% in a matter of weeks. This market crash brought a screeching halt to the merger frenzy.

The Public Utility Holding Company Act of 1935

No industry had been swept away in the mania of the 1920s merger movement quite like the utility industry. As the U.S. population grew and spread out, there was an increasing need for rural, as well as urban power. Utility companies quickly realized that the most efficient way to run their systems was through centralized ownership of power plants and stations. This led to the creation of 'utility holding companies,' in which many utility companies would merge to combine one entity. To illustrate the extent to which the utility mergers occurred, by the end of the decade, within the 18 largest utility firms there existed 42 subholding companies and 91 utility operating companies.

In 1928 the FTC launched a long investigation into the ramifications of the merger wave that had swept the utility industry. It found that the merger movement in the utility industry had resulted in excessive prices for the end consumer. Consequently, the Public Utility Holding Company Act of 1935 was passed into law, requiring the large utility firms to divest themselves of their subsidiaries.

Somewhat ironically, this would have a significantly positive impact on the development of the arbitrage business. As the utilities were forced to sell off their subsidiaries, the subsidiaries initially traded on a when-issued basis. The opportunity for arbitrageurs existed because the when-issued securities traded at a premium to their respective value in the underlying holding company. So, the arbitrageurs began buying the underlying company (pre-split up) and selling short the when issued parts. When the company was actually split up, and the when issued became the actual securities, the long and the short positions would cancel each other out. But the arbitrageur profited because he had sold the parts for more than he had purchased the underlying whole. Along with the recapitalization of the railroads, this was the fundamental development that spawned risk arbitrage in the United States.

The End of the Early Twentieth Century Mergers

The Utility Act was the official response to, and end of, the merger movements that took place in the early 1900s. It was during this early period of economic growth and financial consolidation that arbitrageurs in the United States first had the opportunity to manifest their prowess and create and develop a new form of investment. Following the Great Depression of the 1930s, merger activity slowed into the 1940s and 1950s. In fact, it was not until the conglomeratization of the 1960s that mergers and risk arbitrageurs would once again have their day in the sun.

◆ ◆ ◆

Chapter 3: Merger Waves of the 60s, 80s, 90s

The latter half of the twentieth century has witnessed three distinct waves of mergers. The decade of the 1960s saw the building of corporate conglomerates as companies tried to diversify their income streams. In the 1980s, financial raiders armed with high yield debt went after corporate entities to unlock 'lazy assets.' Finally, in the 1990s, consolidation took place as corporate buyers looked to create synergies and cost savings within their own industry. Each of these three waves created opportunity for the arbitrageur and helped define merger arbitrage as we enter the 21st century.

The First Wave: Conglomerators in the 1960s

The merger wave of the 1960s traces its roots to the studies of two economists, Wesley Mitchell and Arthur Burns. Work by these two in the 1940s and 50s led to widespread acknowledgement of the classic business cycle. Mitchell and Burns exhorted that most industrial nations experienced economic cycles lasting for a period of years in which various sectors of the economy would expand and contract at different rates. In other words, the economy was cyclical.

Corporate managements of the 1960s bought into the Burns/Mitchell ideology. Their response was the launch of a merger wave in which corporations sought to buy companies in unrelated businesses. The thinking was that the parent company could smooth out its earnings stream by owning subsidiaries that operated in industries whose earnings peaked and troughed within different time cycles. Conglomeratization became the buzzword and mania for the merger movement of the 1960s.

As the volume of mergers tripled between the early and late 1960s, there was ample opportunity for the risk arbitrageurs. Deals were plentiful, and the antitrust agencies were less responsive because of the non-overlapping business nature of the new transactions. The arbitrageurs of the time made a lot of money. Among the better remembered acquiring companies to whom they owed their profits were LTV, Gulf and Western, and ITT.

LTV: Jimmy Ling, the Merger King

Jimmy Ling was perhaps the most colorful and imaginative of the 1960s conglomerators. After dropping out of high school at an early age, he started a small electrical contracting business, Ling Electric (later known as LTV). Spurred by a strong economy and steady earnings growth, Ling soon began acquiring other small electronic and defense contractors. His company grew quickly and in the 1960s Ling diversified by acquiring such firms as Braniff Airlines, J&L Steel, and the National Car Rental Company.

By the late 1960s, LTV was the fourteenth largest corporation in the country with annual sales of $3.8 billion. Arbitrageurs had benefited handsomely from the string of acquisitions that had created the new LTV. Many of the acquisitions had been funded with what was known as 'Chinese Paper.' This referred to the unusual means of payment that Ling continually came up with for his corporate purchases. Payment was often a mixture of debt, convertible preferred, common stock, and even cash. While this often made the value of such transactions difficult to ascertain, the arbitrageurs who understood the deals and the securities being used as payment could reap tremendous profits.

Gulf and Western, a.k.a. Engulf and Devour

One of the great corporate acquirers of the decade was Charles Bluhdorn's Gulf and Western (G&W). Due to its acquisition prowess, the company was known on the Street as 'Engulf and Devour.' G&W began as an auto parts manufacturing firm but through acquisition transformed itself into a conglomerate with units in the food, steel, and entertainment businesses. Its reasons for diversification were representative of the time period. Bluhdorn was bored with the staid business of auto parts and its low growth earnings potential. He felt that he could enhance shareholder value by growing through acquisition and diversifying into an assortment of industries.

Similar to Ling's, Bluhdorn's mergers created plentiful opportunity for the arbitrageurs. One such opportunity was the run that G&W took at Sinclair Oil in 1968. With Sinclair stock trading 20 percent below its book value, Bluhdorn took a seven percent stake at about $80 a share and then launched a tender offer for $114 a share. Bluhdorn knew that Sinclair had extremely close relations with Atlantic Richfield and that the two firms had previously considered merging. Because of this, Bluhdorn felt that he would profit on his position even if Atlantic Richfield, rather than his G&W, ended up acquiring Sinclair. Arbitrageurs uncovered this information in the course of researching the G&W bid for Sinclair. Those arbitrageurs that bought Sinclair stock after the G&W tender announcement were rewarded just a few months later when it was announced that Atlantic Richfield would buy Sinclair for $130 a share cash, a 14% premium to Bluhdorn's original offer.

ITT

In 1959, Harold Geneen became president of ITT. At the time, International Telephone & Telegraph's business consisted primarily of small telephone companies located abroad. In an effort to reduce the company's dependence on foreign earnings and diversify its revenue stream, Geneen embarked on a legendary acquisition spree. The companies that ITT bought included Avis Rent-a-Car, Sheraton Hotels, Continental Banking, and Hartford Insurance. In 1968 alone, ITT acquired 20 different concerns.

Geneen's primary acquisition tool was the tender offer. As with most other corporate acquirers, ITT would usually take a small stockholding in the target firm and then launch a 14-day tender offer. It was through this process in the 1960s that the arbitrageurs began playing a pivotal role in the merger and acquisition business. Acquirers like ITT would rely on the fact that arbs would buy up the stock of the target and tender their shares, giving control of the target company to ITT. For assuming the deal risk, the arbitrageurs were usually compensated with a generous return on their investment.

Of course, the returns were not automatic. In 1965, ITT announced that it would merge with ABC, the American Broadcasting Companies. On news of the announcement, ABC stock traded up from $58 a share to about $74 a share. Arbitrageurs bought in to the deal, going long ABC in the mid $70 per share range. The stock continued to trade up as the deal came closer to consummation and soon approached $90. But months later, when the Federal Communications Commission blocked the deal on antitrust grounds, the arbitrage community was crippled. The deal broke, and ABC stock plummeted back to the mid $50 a share range. Such were the perils of arbitrage investing.

The merger wave of the 1960s came to an end in 1968. A confluence of factors combined to stop conglomeratization. When Litton Industries announced its first earnings decrease in fourteen years, people began to question the wisdom of conglomerates. In addition, the antitrust agencies began to more closely scrutinize some transactions. There continued to be opportunity in the arbitrage world, but the pace of mergers abated into the 1970s.

The Second Wave: Hostile Deals in the 1980s

During the decade of Greed is Good, even Broadway picked up on the trend with the late 1980s play, 'Other People's Money.' This production exemplified the merger wars that took place throughout much of the decade. In the play, a corporate raider known as 'Larry the Liquidator' tries to buy a small suburban cable and wire firm. The firm's stock trades at $14 a share and Larry offers to pay $20. He feels that if he can obtain control, he can realize the full $25 value of the firm by selling off the core wire business. Jorgey, the firm's chairman does not want the company to be split up and does not like Larry the Liquidator. Unfortunately for Jorgey, though, Larry is right. The true value of the entity can be realized only through the sale of its parts. Consequently, the firm's shareholders much prefer Larry's $20 a share offer to Jorgey's track record of inactivity and flat returns. As such, the deal is consummated and shareholders profit.[2]

The fictional events portrayed in Other People's Money actually occurred on a much larger scale in many of the deals of the 1980s as financial intermediaries armed with high yield debt went after major corporations. While strategic corporate buyers and foreign multinationals accounted for some of the merger activity, it was the leveraged buyout (LBO) funds like KKR and Forstmann Little, and the corporate raiders like T. Boone Pickens and Carl Icahn that characterized the 1980s buyout binge.

KKR's leveraged buyout of Houdaille Industries in 1979 signified the birth of the LBO fund. It was a $350 million transaction that was financed with 85 percent debt. After the successful completion of the deal, Wall Street became enamored of the profits that could be attained through leveraged acquisitions. With banks like Drexel Burnham Lambert providing the financing, an LBO fund could purchase a company with very little money down, unlock that firm's hidden value by selling off assets, and realize tremendous returns. This began the second merger wave and brought on the heyday of the arbitrageur.

Ivan Boesky

Until this time, the arbitrage community had been relatively unknown. While Guy Wyser-Pratte had published his "Risk Arbitrage" thesis (NYU Graduate School of Business) in the Bulletin of Finance in 1971, arbs were generally not visible outside of the investment world. That changed in the 1980s as arbitrageurs like Ivan Boesky rose to prominence. With a background in law, Boesky began his career on Wall Street as a securities analyst. Bored by the slow pace of equity research, he soon discovered the faster world of risk arbitrage. By late 1975, Boesky had started his own risk arbitrage firm, investing in announced merger deals. He was extremely successful, netting profits of close to $50 million on Texaco's purchase of Getty Oil and over $65 million on the Chevron acquisition of Gulf Oil.[3] As the 1980s deal frenzy increased, arbs like Boesky and Asher Edelman quickly became the glamour figures on Wall Street. As a group, the arbitrageurs epitomized the high-stakes merger and acquisition Wall Street environment.

In his book, *Merger Mania*, published in New York in 1985, Boesky explained that "successful risk arbitrageurs are independent minded and willing to take risks. They generally have renounced the chance to live a more bureaucratic but perhaps less grueling life. There is a thrill to this sort of independence, a certain kind of excitement to putting oneself on the line all the time and trying to come up a winner."[4] And so risk arbitrage was in full swing. Years later, Boesky would be forced out of the business after admitting to charges of insider trading and the arbitrage community would again go into a hiatus. But not until the big deals of the 1980s bore themselves out and the arbitrage community reaped tremendous profits.

The Fight for Macmillan

Of all the 1980s hostile deals, the battle for control of Macmillan, Inc., the large U.S. publishing company, was likely the most profitable for risk arbitrageurs. While it is not as renowned as the famous LBO transaction in which KKR bought RJR Nabisco (later chronicled in the book *Barbarians at the Gate*), the excitement of the saga that unfolded has been compared to that of a Superbowl playoff game. On May 17, 1988, just seven months after the 1987 market crash, Robert Bass, a Texas billionaire active in the M&A game, launched a $64 unsolicited tender offer for the 91% of Macmillan that he did not already own. As arbitrageurs began buying Macmillan stock in anticipation of another hostile 80s-style takeover battle, the stock traded up through $64 a share.

Macmillan responded to Bass's offer with a management-led restructuring plan valued between $65 to $70 a share, including a one-time $50 per share dividend. A few days later, on June 6, Bass raised his offer to $73 and filed a motion in court to block Macmillan management's restructuring. The Delaware Court issued an injunction against the Macmillan restructuring, contending that it forced shareholders to accept a lower value for their holdings. This was typical of the legal climate at the time that facilitated hostile takeovers and in turn gave the arbitrageurs increasing returns. On July 18, Bass raised his offer again to $75 and the arbitrageurs continued buying, pushing Macmillan stock over $78 in anticipation of a still higher bid.

Three days later, the arbs were rewarded as Robert Maxwell, chairman of Maxwell Communications, entered the fray with an $80 cash offer for Macmillan. In the weeks that followed, Bass, Maxwell, and Macmillan management continued to raise the ante against one another until Maxwell finally won out with a $90.25 cash bid for the company. It had been a classic 1980s hostile bidding war in which Macmillan shareholders and the arbitrageurs emerged the true victors.

United Airlines Crash Ends an Era

The end of the 1980s merger wave came with the attempted management-led buyout of United Airlines (UAL). In September of 1989, UAL had announced a $6.75 billion employee buyout of the airline for $300 a share. The stock of UAL quickly traded up to $280 a share as arbitrageurs took positions in what looked like a shaky deal from the start. Growing conservatism on the part of regulators, extremely ambitious projections for the airline going forward, and unsecured financing all contributed to the risk that was inherent in the deal. But the arbitrageurs had been spoiled by the success and relative ease with which they had made money for much of the decade. Reflecting on the UAL deal, William Kaye, head of risk arbitrage at Paine Webber, said that *over the last few years arbs made so much money they were allowed to roam the range...(arbs) threw caution to the wind on (the UAL deal). They wanted to believe it would get done – it would just make their year – so they just said it would get done.*[5]

The buyout was to be financed with $3 billion from UAL's banks, Chase Manhattan and Citicorp, and the remaining $4 billion from a planned credit facility. UAL management was using cash because the junk bond market, a source of much of the financing for the decade's deals, was no longer a viable option. Michael Milken's early 1989 indictment and subsequent resignation from Drexel had dried up all liquidity that had once existed in the junk bond market.

But on Friday the thirteenth of October 1989, the banks announced that they had been unable to secure the $4 billion needed. The reason was that the Japanese banks, from which much of the $4 billion was to come, had pulled out of the financing syndicate because they did not like the deal's fees and structure. As the deal broke, UAL stock fell over $100 a share, back below the $200 level. The arbitrageurs were devastated. Many had been wiped out. Losses in the arbitrage community were estimated to be more than $1 billion. As a result of the UAL collapse, the market had a mini crash with the Dow Jones Industrial Average dropping 200 points (at the time, a significant selloff).

On the day of the crash, our chairman, Mario Gabelli, was playing golf with Bob Farrell of Merrill Lynch at the Quaker Ridge Golf Club. Having the round of his life at two under par, news of the market tumult reached Mario on the course and his game began to falter. Two holes and two double bogies later, Mario and Bob left the course to go into the office and assess the havoc that had been wreaked.

In the months that followed, deal flow dried up and the merger frenzy of the 1980s came to an end. Many marginal players were forced out of the risk arb business and those that were left had to contend with smaller spreads and lower returns due to a slowing of M&A activity. In several years another round of mergers would commence and the risk arbitrageurs would again prevail. However, never again would the risk arbitrage business see the hefty returns that were afforded by the merger mania that swept Wall Street in the 1980s.

The Third Wave: Consolidators in the 1990s

General Electric Sounds the Gong

In the early 1990s there was a lull in merger activity. There were fewer friendly deals and with the exception of a select number of hostile offers, notably AT&T's bid for NCR in 1990, hostile acquisitions had all but ceased to exist. That changed on March 14, 1994 when General Electric made a $2.4 billion hostile bid for Kemper Insurance. Although GE's bid would ultimately fail and the two firms would not merge, its very act changed the way that corporate America viewed mergers and acquisitions.

In 1994, GE and its Chairman Jack Welch were American corporate icons. If Jack Welch was doing hostile deals, then mergers and acquisitions were once again an acceptable means of growth. Gabelli Asset Management heralded to the world that the 'Gong' had sounded, signaling the start of the THIRD WAVE of M&A activity. Wall Street's arbitrage community, which had shrunk considerably during the extended lull in deal activity, was back in business.

Strategic Buyers, Global Players

In the third merger wave (1990s) corporations are combining with competitors in their own industry. The point of the deal is not to diversify as in the 1960s or make a quick profit as raiders did in the 1980s, but rather to extend franchises, cut costs, and improve profitability.

Corporations in the 1990s view mergers as a tool to reposition themselves in a changing and dynamic business environment. The need for scale has become increasingly important. As the merger wave has gathered momentum, companies have had to join in and go full scale or fall back and become niche players. Bigger is better. One plus one can equal three. Global behemoths like Citigroup in the financial sector and Bernie Ebbers' MCI Worldcom in the telecommunications industry have emerged. CEOs like Dennis Kozlowski of Tyco International Ltd. have built up massive corporations through repeated acquisitions.

In fact, big is not only better domestically, but on an international basis as well. The fall of the Berlin Wall in 1989 accelerated the spread of free market economies. This catalyzed cross-border transactions as oil giant British Petroleum acquired Amoco and Daimler Benz merged with Chrysler. These global opportunities have been one of the primary catalysts that have spurred the 90s merger wave.

Another major characteristic of 1990s M&A activity has been the use of equity as acquisition currency. An unprecedented and sustained bull market has brought share prices to dizzying levels, giving acquirers greater purchasing power. In addition, interest rates have been at extremely low levels for most of the 1990s and this has made cash cheap to borrow. Regardless of whether corporate acquirers are using stock or cash, the cost of capital in doing a deal if often quite low, in relative terms.

1990s Arbitrage

Given the resurgence of merger activity, arbitrage is flourishing. But the business has changed from the frenetic pace of the previous decade. Arbitrageurs are no longer associated with the corporate raiders and aggressive LBO firms of the 1980s. Risk arbitrage is now considered a relatively conservative style of investment. While merger arbitrage returns in the 1980s were over 25%, returns today are generally between 10% and 15%. This is in part related to lower interest rates. For example, while long term U.S. Treasury bonds' yields were as high as 13-14% in the 1980s, they have been closer to 6-8% in the 1990s. Hence, relative to these lower rates, 1990s returns are roughly comparable to those of the 1980s. Furthermore, many of today's deals are less risky than those of the 80s. Since 1991, only about 3.5% of the deals announced have been called off. This compares to roughly 7% of such deals being cancelled in the 1980s.[6] With fewer deals falling through, arbitrageurs have accepted a lower return for a lower level of risk.

That is not to say that all deals in the 1990s have been kind to arbitrageurs. 1998 was a particularly difficult year, with the collapse of such deals as American Home Products/Monsanto and Tellabs/Ciena. The failure of these two deals created a major shakeup in the arbitrage community as Monsanto fell from over $60 a share to under $35 and Ciena crashed from over $90 a share to less than $10 in a period of weeks. These and other busted deals provided further incentive for the arbs to invest only in the conservative, simple, and risk-free deals that offered somewhat lower returns.

Another factor impacting arb returns is the renewed popularity of this relatively low-risk strategy for generating consistently positive returns. Many of today's veteran arbs complain that there is too much money chasing arb deals, in the process reducing spreads and potential returns.

By 1998, large funds like Long Term Capital Management (LTCM) had entered the arbitrage business. The entry of such sizable participants in merger arb served to tighten spreads in most deals. However, when several of LTCM's highly leveraged bond investments moved against them in the summer of 1998, the fund's lenders demanded repayment. LTCM was forced to quickly liquidate many of its arb positions, forcing spreads to open quickly. This gave paper losses to any arb involved in the same deals as LTCM, but it created opportunity in the merger arb market by "widening spreads."

This ebb and flow pattern of opening and closing spreads is correlated to the amount of arb oriented money in the business and risk tolerance. Money constantly seeks and flows to the highest perceived level of risk adjusted return. Arbitrageurs enter the business, forcing down returns. As with any business, the more players that exist, the lower the returns are. The cycle begins to turn when deals break, arbs are caught in such deals, suffer losses, and exit the business. This in turn forces returns higher because there are less arbs in the business investing in deals. Those that remain demand a higher return for their risk because they too were hurt in recent broken deals. This forces returns even higher, which again attracts marginal players to the business and the cycle repeats itself. This has been a pattern that has played out several times in the 1990s world of arbitrage. However, for those that diversify against the potential land mines of broken deals, this unprecedented merger wave offers tremendous arbitrage opportunity.

The Financial Accounting Standards Board has recently sought to end the use of pooling accounting in all mergers. In the time before this action is implemented (likely in 2001), there should be a renewed flood of mergers, as companies rush to consolidate while they can still use the pooling accounting rules. Pooling accounting benefits merging companies in that they do not incur goodwill expense, which lowers earnings.

This trend will serve to prolong the incredible 1990s wave of mergers. Coming on the heels of 1960s conglomeratization and 1980s hostile raids, the 1990s have provided arbs with a merger cycle that should last for many years to come. The charts and tables on the next page illustrate the tremendous merger activity that has fueled arbitrage in recent years. Regardless of when the current crescendo ends, merger activity will continue to ebb and flow, as it has for the past 40 years. And as long as it flows more than it ebbs, the arbitrageurs will generate solid non market correlated returns.

Flow of Funds

Sources ($)	1994	1995	1996	1997	1998
U.S. Deals	$340	$511	$652	$919	$1,620
Stock Buybacks	46	99	176	181	207
Mutual Fund Purchases	119	125	222	232	159
Dividends	182	205	262	275	279

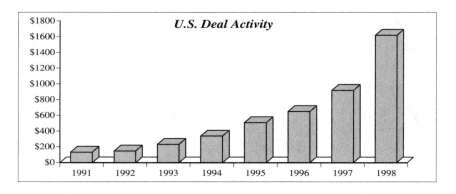

Deal Activity

	1994	1995	1996	1997	1998
Worldwide	$575	$950	$1,140	$1,600	$2,453
U.S. Total	340	511	652	919	1,620
U.S. Cash	212	254	356	450	549

Deal

	1996	1997	1998
U.S. Deals (in billions)	$652	$919	$1,620
Number of Transactions	5,848	7,800	7,758
Average Size (in millions)	$114	$118	$203

◆ ◆ ◆

Chapter 4: Risk and Return - The Spread

More than 2000 Years ago, a Greek writer named Antipater of Sidon compiled a list of what he considered to be the most spectacular buildings of his day. These later became widely known as the Seven Wonders of the World.

This chapter will discuss the risk vs. return issues that face the arbitrageur. When a merger deal is announced, the arbitrageur weighs the return he stands to earn versus the risk that the deal entails. The return earned is the 'spread' between the deal value and the price at which the target company (the company being bought) is trading at in the public marketplace. His risk is twofold: first, that of non-consummation of the deal, and how far the target stock will fall in such an event; second, how long the deal will take and what happens if there are snags that stretch out the closing of the deal. After considering the issues on both sides, the arb will invest in the spreads and deals that offer the highest rate of return with the lowest risk. We explain below the various components that comprise the return and the different issues that account for risk in a merger deal.

Return

In determining the return on a particular deal, the arbitrageur must first ascertain the value of the deal. In most deals, the currency used to pay for the target company will be either cash, stock of the acquirer, or a combination of the two.

In a cash transaction, it is quite simple. The value of the deal is constant and equals the cash price offered by the acquirer. When Lufthansa offered to buy Hudson General for $76/share cash, the value of the offer was $76.

In a stock for stock transaction, the value of the deal will fluctuate with the price of the buyer's stock. For example, AT&T offered to buy McCaw Cellular Communications in 1993 in a one share for one share stock swap. This meant that when the deal closed, shareholders of McCaw would receive one share of AT&T for each McCaw share they owned. From the time the offer was made to the time the deal closed, the value of the deal for McCaw shareholders fluctuated with the price at which AT&T's stock was trading. With AT&T's stock at $60/share, the value of the deal for McCaw's shareholders was $60/share. If AT&T fell to $50, the value of the deal was $50. The value of the deal moved with and was always equal to the price of AT&T stock.

Because there is always some risk of non-consummation, Hudson General will trade at a price below $76/share and McCaw will trade at a price below that of AT&T's stock. *The difference between the value of the deal and the price at which the target company trades is known as 'the spread'.* The spread is probably the most common term used on a risk arbitrage trading desk and is the number upon which arb returns are based. The arbitrageur will earn the spread on a deal, and hence his return is the spread divided by his investment.

If the arb buys Hudson General at $74/share in the open market, then receives $76/share when the deal closes, his profit is the $2 spread ($76/share received minus $74/share cost). His return is the $2/share earned divided by the $74/share invested, or 2.7%. This is an extremely simplified example. In reality, several other factors also play into the calculation of the return. Four of the more important factors are timing, cost of capital, dividends, and taxes.

Timing

The time value of money concept plays a pivotal role in the calculation of return to the arbitrageur. Rather than looking at the 2.7% overall return that was earned in the Hudson General example, an arb will focus on the annualized return of a particular deal. The annualized return is determined by the length of time it takes for the deal to close. An arbitrageur must estimate when the merger will be complete and when will he get his money from the buyer.

If the Hudson General merger closed one month after the arb bought his stock at $74, his 2.7% return would equate to an annualized return of 32.4%. However, if the deal dragged on for whatever reason, and took 8 months to close, the 2.7% would equate to an annualized return of only 4.1%. Based on this example, it is clear that the time it takes for a deal to close is extremely important for the arbitrageur.

The two primary factors affecting timing in a deal are the regulatory approval time frame and the SEC approval of the proxy statement in a tender offer.

Merger

Regulatory Approval	Federal Trade Commission or the Department of Justice has 30 days to review and approve or disallow a merger. While that is the guideline, it may take longer, particularly if a second request is issued to the companies for additional information.
SEC – Proxy Approval	The SEC takes approximately one month to approve the preliminary proxy statement issued by the merging companies.
Shareholder Vote	Once the companies receive proxy approval, they mail the proxy to shareholders and set the date for the shareholder vote on the merger – vote is usually held about 1 month after proxy approval.
Merger Close	Most mergers will typically close within 3 months of being announced, as long as the above processes go smoothly.

Tender Offer

Regulatory Approval	FTC or DOJ has 15 days to review and approve or disallow a tender offer.
Tender Timing	Tender offer must be open for a minimum of 20 business days.
Tender Close	A tender will typically be completed within 1 month of being announced, as long as the above processes go smoothly.

Cost of Capital

The arb's cost of capital is the rate he will have to pay on the money he borrows to invest. This is known as the broker call rate and is the arb's financing cost. In the Hudson General example, if the broker call rate was 5%, and the deal closed in one month, the arb would have to pay (5% / 12 months) on the $74 he borrowed to invest. This would have cost the arb 0.4%, reducing his overall return from 2.7% to 2.3%.

In the same manner in which the arb considers the borrow cost he will pay on his investment, he also takes into account the credit he will receive on his short position. In a stock-for-stock transaction, the arb will sell short the acquirer's stock and purchase the target to lock in a spread. The arb will be paid interest on his short position, as he is in essence loaning out funds by being short.

Dividends

An arbitrageur will also account for any dividends that will be received on the target stock before the closing of the deal. In the Hudson General deal, an arbitrageur would have bought Hudson General stock and would thus be entitled to receive any dividends the company paid. If Hudson General paid a $0.25/share dividend in the period that the arb was long the stock, the above mentioned spread would increase from $2 to $2.25, a 12.5% increase in the return.

By the same token, the arb must deduct any dividends that are paid out on the acquirer's stock. Because the arb sells short the acquirer's stock, he is required to pay any dividends that are issued on that stock during the period that he is short. In the AT&T deal, arbs were short AT&T and long McCaw, thus having to pay any dividends on AT&T, and receiving dividends on McCaw. The payment of dividends can greatly reduce the spread and return on a stock for stock deal. Because of that, it is an important part of the return analysis.

Taxes

As with any investment, taxes are an important factor in the calculation of return to the arbitrageur. The transaction can be taxed at two levels. First, the merger itself usually results in a taxable exchange to the shareholder if it is a cash deal. On the other hand, most stock-for-stock deals are structured so that they are tax-free. Second, the shareholder is then taxed on the capital gain that is realized. Because most mergers are consummated in a period of time less than one year, the arb is usually taxed at the short-term capital gains rate. This makes arb returns more attractive for tax deferred type vehicles such as a 401k.

Risk

As we explained in Chapter 1, the premise behind risk arbitrage is that it generates very consistent returns with rarely a down year. The eighth wonder of the world is compound interest and the key to compounding is to not break the chain by having a down year. A good risk arbitrageur will seldom have a year in which money is lost. So what is the risk in risk arbitrage?

The primary risk is that the merger, upon which the arbitrageur has placed his bet, does not go through. Keep in my mind that in an average deal an arb may stand to make only 2 to 5% on the upside of the investment (if the deal is consummated), but usually risks 20-50% downside if the deal falls apart. *More than one observer of the arb world has quipped that arbitrage is a business in which you risk dollars to make nickels.* On the face of things, these do not sound like odds that the intelligent investor would want. But an arbitrageur will diversify his risk among many deals, so that if one falls apart, it accounts for only a small percent of his portfolio. While diversification minimizes risk, it is still of paramount importance for an arb to avoid deals that blow up. Let's look at an example.

Broken Deal

ABC is trading in the market at $11/share. On March 1, Buyer Co. announces that it has entered into an agreement with ABC to buy all of its outstanding common stock at $15/share in cash. Assume that it looks like a fairly safe deal, and when the market opens, the arbs start buying ABC at $14.75/share. The logic on the part of the arbs is as follows: buy the stock at $14.75 and when the deal closes (let's say one month from now), the arb will get $15/share cash. In one month's time the arb will make $0.25/share, a return of 1.7%. If this return is annualized, however, and the arb makes 1.7% every month for a year, he will realize an annualized gain of 20.4%.

Not all mergers are consummated so smoothly. The major risk here is that the deal does not close. This can happen for several reasons, which we will explain later. For now, assume that the two firms have an irreconcilable disagreement over some issue and decide to terminate the merger. When the market next opens for trading, ABC plummets back down to its pre-merger level because it is no longer going to be sold and business is as it was before Buyer Co. came along. The stock of ABC opens at $11/share. The arbitrageur, meanwhile, is still long ABC and now has an unrealized loss on the stock he bought at $14.75 of $3.75, or 25.4%. Risk vs. return. 1.7% upside vs. 25.4% downside.

This example is meant to illustrate just one point. On each deal, the arbitrageur's upside is rather small and the downside quite significant. Several broken deals can severely damage the returns of a risk arbitrage fund. The extent to which an arbitrageur is correct in anticipating the outcome of a deal is what really drives the returns of any arb fund. If the arb can avoid broken deals, the 1.7% returns add up to a significant annual yield.

February 28	ABC trades in open market at $11/share.
March 1	Buyer Co. bids $15/share for all ABC common stock.
March 2	ABC opens for trading at $14.75/share as arbs purchase stock.
March 13	Buyer Co. announces that it has withdrawn its offer.
March 14	ABC falls and opens for trading at $11/share.
	Arbs lose $3.75/share on ABC stock.

What Can Go Wrong

Having shown the importance of knowing that a deal will be completed, it follows that an arbitrageur must know what can go wrong. These issues are outlined in the arbitrage check list/decision tree in Appendix I. The following commentary addresses some of the most common causes of a failed merger attempt:

Regulatory Issues

Most deals that do not close are due to problems in getting the merger approved by the various regulatory commissions. The Hart-Scott-Rodino Antitrust Improvements Act of 1976 required that the Department of Justice (DOJ) or the Federal Trade Commission (FTC) approve any merger or corporate acquisition before consummation. The combining firms must give notification to the two antitrust agencies and will receive a ruling within fifteen days for a cash tender or thirty days for other forms of transactions as to whether the proposed merger violates antitrust laws.

The purpose of this process is to prevent the creation of a merged entity that will have considerable dominance over an industry or sector. Because the FTC and DOJ can block such mergers, arbitrageurs prefer to invest in deals in which the two merging entities have little overlap in specific businesses. The greater the overlap, the higher the chance that the merger will be blocked by the DOJ or the FTC.

In addition to the FTC and DOJ, certain mergers may need approval from their respective industry regulatory boards. For example, mergers in the communications industry must be approved by the Federal Communications Commission and utility mergers require the approval of the Federal Energy Regulatory Commission. The role of the regulatory agencies is discussed further in Chapter 8.

Due Diligence

It is important for an arbitrageur to find out whether or not the buyer has completed its due diligence review on the seller. Sometimes a deal will fall through because as the buyer gets further into the due diligence process, it discovers something about the target that it does not like. This could be anything from accounting irregularities to a lack of strategic fit. If the buyer becomes uncomfortable with what it is buying, the deal could fall through or the price may be renegotiated lower. In either case, the target stock will trade down and the arbitrageur will lose money.

Financing

A potential pitfall in the consummation of a cash transaction is the lack of financing to fund the payment. A deal is safest from a financing standpoint if the funding has already been secured from the banks or if the company already has the available cash. The arb must ask if the buyer has a commitment from the banks or the credit facility from which it will obtain funds. The more secure this commitment is, the less likely it is that the deal will fall through because of financing issues.

Hostile Deal

If a hostile takeover is being attempted, management of the target company may not want to sell. Possible defenses include the poison pill, staggered boards, and other shark repellents. These are discussed in Chapter 10. The point is, though, that if a deal is hostile, there is a greater risk that the buyer will be forced to abandon its efforts to acquire its target company. If the target management is persistent in its attempt to remain independent, it is very difficult to consummate a merger deal.

Shareholder Vote

The shareholder vote is usually not a difficult issue, because most mergers are completed at a significant premium to the target stock's pre-merger price. However, the arbitrageur must find out if there are any issues that could possibly prevent the required majority of shareholders to vote in favor of the deal. If there are issues that will cause a split in the shareholders' interests, the arbitrageur looks at the percent of the shareholder vote required for merger completion and the likelihood that the acquirer will receive its threshold vote.

Fall in Buyer's Stock Price

Although merger arbitrage is considered a 'market neutral' style of investing, significant moves in the price of the buyer's stock can affect the terms of the merger or the merger itself. For example, when AT&T announced that it would buy McCaw in a one-for-one stock swap, AT&T's stock price was at $60/share. McCaw shareholders were to receive one share of AT&T, a $60 value for each share they owned. However, if AT&T stock had fallen to $30/share before the deal closed, McCaw shareholders may no longer have been interested in a deal that now gave them only $30/share of value.

A Real Life Busted Deal: Staples/Office Depot

Staples/Office Depot was the classic 'busted deal' of the 1990's that caused pain in the arbitrage community. On September 4, 1996, Staples announced that it would buy Office Depot in a 1.14 to 1 stock swap. The arbitrage community immediately began to invest in the deal by buying Office Depot, shorting Staples, and locking in the approximate $3 spread. In the months that followed, the FTC requested additional information from the companies and extended its regulatory review process. It became evident that the FTC had considerable reservations about the proposed combination from an antitrust perspective. The FTC was concerned because the combination of the two firms would result in an entity with a significant share of the office supplies market.

As speculation about possible non-consummation of the deal circulated, the spread fluctuated wildly for months. Some surmised that the FTC would just force Office Depot to sell certain stores, but allow the deal to go through. Other arbs felt that the FTC would block the deal, and unwound their positions at a small loss. In April 1997, the FTC announced that it would seek a preliminary injunction against the deal. ODP immediately plunged from $21/share to about $13/share, leaving the arbitrageurs with big losses. The FTC commissioners overruled their staff, which had actually voted in favor of the merger.

With the spread having widened and with Office Depot at such a low price, many arbs doubled up and invested more in the deal, betting that the preliminary injunction would not stop the merger. The matter went to a federal court where Office Depot and Staples squared off against the FTC. In July of that year the court ruled in favor of the FTC and barred the merger. Office Depot fell again and the arbs lost more money.

Office Depot traded down $4.50 a share to $15. Most arbs dumped the stock, realizing losses of close to 25% for the second time in a matter of months. Interestingly, the $15 a share level at which many arbs panicked and sold the stock was the low tick at which Office Depot would trade for years to come. Had an arbitrageur focused on the fundamentals of ODP, holding onto the stock could have generated a significant return. (But this is generally not the rule in the arb community. If a deal busts, move the stock out and move on!)

The point of discussing this deal is to highlight the risks involved in merger arbitrage. For every Staples/Office Depot merger that is not completed, there are many more that are. By spreading risk among many deals, the prudent arbitrageur will mitigate such inevitable pitfalls and deliver consistent returns.

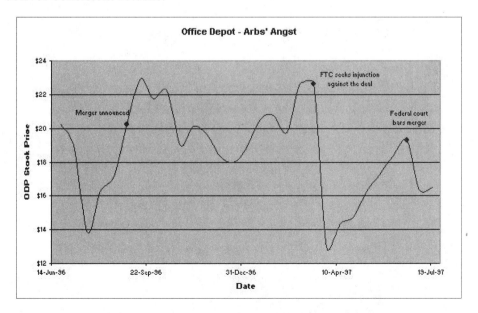

Chapter 5: Neutrogena - Analysis of a Deal

The Pyramids (2580 BC). The largest and most impressive is the Great Pyramid at Giza. It took thousands of men about 30 years to build and is the only one of the seven ancient wonders that still stands today.

This chapter will walk you through the actual thought process that an arbitrageur would have undertaken in the analysis of a typical deal: the Johnson & Johnson-Neutrogena merger in 1994. There is a checklist (See Appendix I) an arbitrageur runs through to ascertain the risk and the potential returns of a deal. Much like an airline pilot does before take-off, an arb gains a level of comfort that the deals in which he invests will indeed be consummated.

On August 22, 1994, Johnson & Johnson, a leading international health care corporation, announced that it had reached an agreement to buy Neutrogena, a specialty hair and skin care products firm. J&J would buy all of Neutrogena's outstanding common shares for $35.25 per share. The deal would take place in the form of a cash tender offer that would be launched immediately and last for 20 business days. This was a typical cash tender offer that would draw the attention of arbitrageurs. Upon seeing the announcement, the arbitrage analyst would quickly begin his analysis by attempting to answer the following questions.

Preliminary Questions

What is the Deal Spread?

First things first. Is there a spread that would provide the arbitrageur with a reasonable return if he did invest in the deal? On release of the merger news, Neutrogena stock opened at $34.75 per share. This left a spread between the current market price of $34.75 and the $35.25 deal price of $0.50 per share. The fifty-cent return on the $34.75 investment equaled 1.4%. This meant that if the deal closed in just one month's time, an arbitrageur would realize an annualized return of 16.8%. Given the attractiveness of such a return, an arbitrageur would next want to weigh the risk involved in the deal. If the risks were minimal, he would buy Neutrogena stock at $34.75. The risk analysis begins with the following questions:

Who are the Buyer and Seller?

The first question an arb analyst will ask is, 'Is the deal between buyer and seller a friendly one?' In this case, it was friendly, with the boards of both companies agreeing to merge. This was important to the arbitrageur because it eliminated potential deal breakers like unfriendly target management. Friendly deals, in which both parties have agreed to merge, are more likely to be consummated than hostile takeovers. Because this deal was friendly, it brought a degree of safety to consummation of the merger.

The analyst next considers the identity of the buyer and the seller. J&J is considered a blue-chip company - a leader in its industry with a solid reputation and a proven track record. This again brought comfort to the arbitrageur. *A blue-chip company that is an industry leader is not likely to announce a deal and then back down from it.* These kinds of successful corporations have earned their reputations by avoiding such pitfalls for many years. The better the reputation of the buyer, the more likely it is that the deal will be completed.

Neutrogena was a small company, with a pre-deal market capitalization of $500 million, but a brand name that was well known in moisturizers and specialty soaps. It was this brand name that really spurred J&J's interest in the deal.

A final aspect of the company analysis was the size of the two companies relative to one another. J&J had 1993 sales of over $14 billion while Neutrogena's were less than $300 million. This gave further assurance that the deal would not be difficult for J&J to complete, because the acquisition would be quite a small one for J&J.

What is the Strategic Rationale?

The arbitrageur wants to know if the deal makes strategic sense. Neutrogena had been through a difficult period in the past five years. Its earnings had peaked five years earlier, in 1989, and its stock had fallen nearly 50% since that time. Neutrogena lacked the ubiquitous marketing power and distribution capabilities of bigger firms like Procter & Gamble and Unilever NV. Thus, Neutrogena stood to benefit greatly by coming under the wing of a well-capitalized parent company like J&J.

J&J, meanwhile, wanted to broaden its line of consumer products. Adding the brand name of a company like Neutrogena would enhance its current product line. Furthermore, J&J's distribution channels and marketing strengths would likely help to increase Neutrogena's sales.

For these reasons, the deal made strategic sense. Strategic sense created safety for the arbitrageur (from the standpoint of the deal closing) because both firms stood to benefit. If the deal made sense and would help both companies, it was likely that management would do whatever was necessary to ensure that the deal would get done.

What is the Background of the Deal? (The 14D-1)

To ascertain the background and other details of a deal, arbs will scrutinize certain documents that must be filed with the SEC within five days of a public announcement of a tender offer. In particular, they carefully read through Schedule 14D-1, which must be filed by the potential buyer, and Schedule 14D-9, which the seller must file. These documents contain detailed accounts of the events leading up to the merger agreement and of the players that were involved. Altogether, these documents bring out many of the behind-the-scenes details.

Additional sources of publicly available information include annual reports, '1OK' and '1OQ' filings, and proxy statements. For further insights, arbitrageurs will talk to both companies as well as to the investment bankers who put together the deal. In some cases, lawyers involved with the transaction also will be interviewed. Based on such research, this picture of the J&J-Neutrogena negotiations emerged:

Lloyd Cotsen, chairman and CEO of Neutrogena, had hired Lehman Brothers in early 1994 to explore strategic alternatives to enhance shareholder value. In June of 1994, Lehman Brothers bankers contacted and set up meetings with four consumer products companies (potential acquirers) to discuss the possible sale of Neutrogena. One of them was J&J, and in July of 1994 J&J responded that it would be interested in entering into negotiations to buy Neutrogena. Negotiations lasted several weeks and on August 22 it was announced that a deal, contingent upon regulatory approval and a majority of shares being acquired, had been reached between J&J and Neutrogena.

The importance of the background information for the arbitrageur was twofold. First, it explained the background of the announced transaction and that gave the arb familiarity with the situation. There were no background issues thus far that would cause concern on the part of the arbitrageur. Second, it was important for the arb to know that there had been other parties that were interested. The merger document had read

> *The Company (Neutrogena) and Lehman Brothers received various indications of interest in acquiring the Company from third parties. However, the Company received no offers to acquire the Company from any of the third parties. In addition, none of the third parties indicated an interest in pursuing a transaction which would provide the Company's stockholders with a price for their shares comparable to the price range then being discussed with (J&J).*[7]

This news indicated that there were other interested buyers of Neutrogena. With other buyers in the wings, even if Neutrogena could not complete the J&J deal, it would likely be bought by some firm. This gave the arbs another degree of safety in owning Neutrogena stock. On the other hand, the above passage indicates that the other buyers were below in price to what J&J was willing to pay, so there would be some downside in Neutrogena stock if the deal with J&J were not completed.

Deal Breakers – or the Outs

At this point, the arbitrageur is familiar with the background of the deal, the reason for the merger, the identity of the players, and the return he stands to earn. What he must do next is determine the conditions that could potentially derail the merger. While these may vary from deal to deal, three primary concerns are usually regulatory issues, due diligence, and financing.

While regulatory issues and business overlaps can often keep a merger from going through, they were not a problem in this deal. The only regulatory condition that needed to be satisfied was approval from the Federal Trade Commission under the Hart-Scott-Rodino Antitrust Act. Neutrogena was such a small player in the business of health and beauty aids that it was all but certain that the FTC would approve the merger. This was a major positive for deal safety on the arbitrageur's checklist. On September 19, just three weeks after launching the tender, J&J announced that the required waiting period under the Hart-Scott Act had expired, granting it regulatory approval to acquire Neutrogena.

Is Due Diligence Complete?

The question for the arb to ask here was if J&J had completed its evaluation of Neutrogena, inspected Neutrogena's books, and was comfortable with what it was buying. This due diligence had already been completed, much to the arbitrageur's delight. If J&J had not yet finished its evaluation of Neutrogena, and the deal was contingent upon what J&J found in such an inspection, it would have brought an element of risk to final consummation of the deal.

Show Me the Money - Is Financing an Issue?

Show me the money. The arb wants to find out how the deal will be paid for and if the funding is already in place. Did J&J have enough cash on hand to pay for the acquisition? Would J&J need to increase its debt level by borrowing to fund the acquisition? Were any loans that J&J needed to complete the transaction secured?

In this instance, J&J was paying $924 million in cash to buy Neutrogena. J&J said that it would pay for half the acquisition by using part of its $687 million in cash on its balance sheet. The other half would be paid for through short-term loans, which had already been lined up and secured. Again, due to Neutrogena's small size relative to J&J, and the fact that the money was already secured, financing would not be an issue.

With these three potential concerns alleviated, the arb analyzing the Neutrogena deal would consider some final facts:

Multiple Being Paid

An arbitrageur wants to know if the transaction is fairly valued. In almost all cases, the target company will obtain a fairness opinion from an investment bank that the price for which it is being sold is 'fair,' or in line with other such transactions taking place at that time. This means that based on its selling price, the target company's multiple of earnings or EBITDA, is comparable to that of other companies in its industry or other industry transactions of similar size.

In this case, the price at which Neutrogena was being sold was expensive. At $35.25 per share, J&J was paying 29 times expected 1995 earnings per share of $1.22 and almost 3 times expected sales. Because this price was a big premium to the level at which Neutrogena's competitors traded and the price at which recent similar transactions had gone through, it was unlikely that a competing bid would surface. In addition, it caused angst among arbitrageurs as the downside in Neutrogena stock would be significant if the deal were to fall apart and Neutrogena resumed trading on its fundamentals. The high price that J&J was paying was probably the riskiest element of the deal for arb investors.

Shareholder Vote (Tender)

Sometimes, an acquirer will attempt to buy a percent of the outstanding shares before the merger announcement, in an effort to 'lock up' those votes in favor of the merger. But in this case, there was little concern that enough shareholders would accept the deal. Neutrogena CEO Lloyd Cotsen controlled nearly 10 million shares, over 38% of the total outstanding, directly and through family members. He had agreed to sell all of those shares to J&J at the $35.25 tender price. Thus, J&J needed only to acquire 13% of the shares in the tender to acquire the majority of the outstanding stock and have the deal go through. Considering that Neutrogena had been trading in the low $20s range before the agreement, it was likely that the company's shareholders would embrace the deal and tender their shares.

In the event that the deal was called off, J&J was to receive a $25 million fee plus another $2.5 million for reimbursed expenses. Typically, termination fees are around 2% of the deal price. Here, the $27.5 million total was nearly 3% of the $924 million deal price, so the termination fee was substantial.

Such a fee had two effects. One, it made it very expensive for Neutrogena to back out. Therefore, the likelihood of the deal going through was enhanced. Two, the presence of a termination fee made it more expensive, and therefore less likely, that Neutrogena would receive other offers. Aside from J&J, any company that bought Neutrogena would have assumed the extra $27.5 million obligation as well. In effect, this obligation increased the price a third party would have had to pay.

The Deal Looks Safe

After considering all of this information, the arbitrageur would have decided that the deal looked quite safe, with little risk of non-consummation. You had a bluest of the blue-chips buyer, with financing in place and due diligence complete, no regulatory concerns due to the small size of Neutrogena, a very willing seller in Lloyd Cotsen, and an attractive spread.

Obviously, not all of this information was available immediately to the arbitrage community. The morning that any deal is announced, the arbitrageurs will not have the merger document and will probably have very limited access to management. Many of their questions will be answered on the merger conference call, which is usually conducted the morning of the announcement. Attaining the answers to those questions that are not addressed is what separates the good arbs from the less talented.

Those arbitrageurs that did invest in this deal were rewarded for doing so. The deal closed on September 26, and the arbs received $35.25 in cash just one month after the initial announcement of the tender. Below are the calculations on the return that an arb investor would have realized.

The Math

Buy Neutrogena Shares at	$34.75
Receive in Tender Offer	$35.25
Spread ($35.25-$34.75)	$0.50
Return ($0.50/$34.75)	1.44%
Holding Period (Aug 22-Sep 26)	35 Calendar Days
Annualized Return	15%

Arbs made a profit that was nominally small but attractive on an annualized basis. By asking the right questions, the Neutrogena arbitrageur obtained a level of comfort that allowed him to invest and reap the rewards. Other times, by asking the right questions, an arbitrageur will foresee deal problems and avoid the significant losses associated with investing in deals that go bust. By proceeding carefully and doing the correct analysis, as described above, merger arbitrageurs will generate consistent returns while minimizing risks. A conservative investor's paradise.

◆ ◆ ◆

Chapter 6: Common Deals

The Hanging Gardens of Babylon (9th Century BC). Legend grew of an earthly paradise rising out of the ground...

The Tender - All Cash

In a cash tender offer, an acquirer offers to pay cash for all or part of the outstanding stock of another corporation. The acquirer offers to buy shares of the target company at a fixed price. Most cash tender offers are outstanding for twenty business days and the deal, under current regulatory rules, will usually close within thirty to forty-five days of the tender offer announcement. Because they occur in such a short time frame, annualized returns to the arbitrageur can be quite high, but a decision to participate or not in the deal must be made quickly.

Companies will use a tender offer as a means to merge for one of several reasons. One obvious advantage is the short time frame in which a deal can be completed. A multi-billion dollar acquisition can close quickly. This is advantageous for both parties, as months of haggling with regulatory agencies and merger issues are condensed into a four-week period. In addition, the short time frame will often keep other parties from entering the fray with competing bids for the target. Finally, the firms can simply proceed as a combined entity much sooner than they could have had they done a merger (rather than tender).

Another major reason an acquirer will choose to do a tender offer is to make a hostile bid for a target company that is an unwilling seller. Remember that a tender offer can result from friendly negotiations between a target and a suitor, or it may be unsolicited and hostile. The hostile tender became a favorite tool of the corporate raiders in the 1980s. When a target company is unwilling to agree to merge, a would-be acquirer can put the target 'in play' via a tender offer. Many times this will force the target's management to negotiate.

As an example of a cash tender, consider ITT Industries' acquisition of Goulds Pumps in 1997. On April 21of that year, ITT made a $37 per share tender offer for all the outstanding common stock of Goulds Pumps. The offer was a whopping 62% premium over Goulds' previous day's closing price of $22⅝.

ITT was buying Goulds Pumps in an effort to strengthen its already successful pumps business. By doing so, it would lessen its dependence on the more cyclical aerospace and auto parts businesses which generated two-thirds of its earnings. By buying Goulds, ITT would expand its presence in the water pump business, a business with much higher growth prospects and earnings predictability than auto parts. It would be a small acquisition for ITT but would add meaningfully to top and bottom line growth rates.

ITT had initiated the negotiation process back on March 25. After being rebuffed by Goulds' management in its efforts to meet to discuss a proposal, ITT's chairman and CEO sent a private letter to Goulds management with the following opening statement:

> *I was disappointed that you have continued your unwillingness to meet with us to discuss our proposal. Since we are not able to meet in person...I am sending this letter. ITT Industries, Inc. proposes to acquire Goulds Pumps, Incorporated through a negotiated merger transaction in which Goulds stock-holders would receive $34 in cash for each share of outstanding common stock.*[8]

This letter, which was kept private between management of the two corporations, brought Goulds to the bargaining table. About one month later a friendly cash tender agreement for $37 per share, or $815 million in cash plus the assumption of $119 million in Goulds debt, was announced publicly.

The cash tender would commence on April 25, four days after the announcement, and be in effect for twenty business days. This time frame was standard for a cash tender. The tender offer was expected to be completed in June. This was probably conservative, and in fact, the deal closed even sooner, on May 22.

The day that the tender was announced, arbitrageurs began buying Goulds stock at $36.25 per share. Because they were to receive $37 per share from ITT in one month, they locked in a return of 2.1%, or 25% annualized. This was an extremely attractive return and existed for a reason. There was some overlap in the pump operations and so it was feared that there might be some antitrust concerns on the part of the regulatory commissions. If the combined entity would account for too large a percent of the pump market, it was possible that the antitrust agencies could block the deal, sending Goulds back down to its pre-merger price of $23 per share. For assuming this risk, the arbs were compensated with a potential annualized return of 25%.

Other conditions for completion of the deal also existed. Goulds had business interests in both Italy and Canada, and hence had to comply with the respective regulatory commissions of those countries. In addition, the offer was contingent upon receipt of greater than 50% of Goulds shareholders tendering their stock. The shareholder vote was not seen as a potential problem due to the 62% premium that ITT was paying. On a positive note, due diligence on the part of ITT had been completed and the financing was in place.

On May 21, ITT announced that all applicable waiting periods under the Hart-Scott-Rodino Act in the United States and the Canadian Competition Act in Canada had expired. That is, all necessary regulatory approval for the merger had been attained. As scheduled, the tender expired on May 22, twenty business days after being launched, and the deal was consummated. The arbitrageurs received their money in less than a month's time, realizing annual returns of over 25%. If only all deals were as "Classic" as ITT's cash tender offer for Goulds Pumps.

Cash Mergers

As with cash tenders, this type of deal is for all cash. However, no public tender offer is made to the shareholders of the target. Instead, existing shareholders are given the opportunity to vote on an offer. If the required vote is obtained (the required percent is usually stated in the merger document and is usually over 50%), the merger has been 'approved' by shareholders. Barring any other issues, the shareholders will then receive the cash per share amount that was offered by the acquirer.

Under the Hart-Scott-Rodino Antitrust Act, the required waiting period for clearance from the Justice Department or Federal Trade Commission for mergers is thirty days. Because the waiting period for cash tender offers is only fifteen days their consummation is a much speedier process.

The time frame for a cash merger is also longer than that for a tender offer because of the pre-requisite shareholder vote. Consequently, cash mergers usually take 90 to 120 days to close. In some industries, such as the utility sector, mergers can take a year or longer to be completed. Why should a company choose a merger rather than a tender? The acquirer may need additional time to secure the financing for the deal or to complete its due diligence on the target. If the buyer thinks that this will take longer than a month, it will do a merger rather than a tender. For example, a utility or an insurance company, which needs the approval of its respective industry regulatory agencies, could not possibly obtain that approval in the time frame required by a tender. So deals in those industries will rarely be in the form of a tender, but rather a merger. Similarly, if a company feels that its proposed deal will bring close scrutiny from the Federal Trade Commission or the Department of Justice, it will proceed with a merger rather than tender so that there is ample time to receive the regulatory approval. Such was the case when Procter & Gamble bought Tambrands in 1997.

Procter & Gamble Buys Tambrands in Cash Merger

On April 9, 1997, Procter & Gamble announced that it had entered into a cash merger with Tambrands Inc. to buy all of its outstanding common stock for $50 per share, or $1.85 billion. Procter felt that with its distribution channels and marketing expertise it could greatly leverage the brand name of Tambrands. The deal was a friendly merger, with both parties expected to benefit from the transaction. Procter would add a well-known brand name to its product line and Tambrands shareholders would receive a cash premium, albeit small, to the recent price at which Tambrands had been trading.

On the day that the merger was announced, arbs bought Tambrands stock at around $48 per share, locking in the $2 spread between $48 and the $50 offer price, or a return of 4.2%. Given that the merger was expected to close three months out, the annualized return was approximately 17%. But in the weeks that followed, Tambrands traded down to as low as $46 per share as antitrust concerns caused widespread worries in the arbitrage community. Procter already controlled 41% of the U.S. tampon and sanitary pad market, and the addition of Tambrands would make Procter far and away the largest operator in that industry.

In May, Procter announced that the Justice Department was carefully scrutinizing the deal and approval could take another three to six months. Tambrands stock price adjusted to reflect the new timetable of the merger. Down from $48 to $46 now and with six months to closing, the current four dollar spread ($50-$46) was still an annualized return of 16% (close to the original 17%). But, given the extended time period, the annualized return for any arb who had bought Tambrands at $48, was now only 8%. Such are the perils of arbitrage investing.

Two months later though, in July, Procter announced that it had received over 80% of the regulatory approvals needed from the various countries, including the U.S., and was confident that the remaining would be granted very shortly. Procter was successful in doing so and the deal closed on July 21, just over three months after its initial announcement. Arbs who owned Tambrands stock were well rewarded with a timely close. Those who had bought Tambrands at $46 in May realized an even greater profit – an annualized return of 52%!

Stock-For-Stock Mergers

Stock-for-stock mergers became the deal of choice for corporate buyers in the 1990s. As the stock market boom had brought companies' shares to lofty valuations, it became cheap for these companies to pay for acquisitions with their own stock. When an acquirer feels that its shares are richly valued, it makes much more sense to use equity as currency rather than cash. Another reason for stock-for-stock mergers is that such exchanges are tax-free to shareholders, whereas in a cash merger shareholders must pay capital gains taxes on their realized gain. Finally, in contrast to cash transactions, stock-for-stock mergers may enable the combining companies to use the 'pooling method' of accounting since pooling eliminates the creation of goodwill, which lowers earnings.

Stock mergers are more complicated. Unlike a cash merger where the arbitrageur will just buy the target stock, in a stock merger an arbitrageur will buy the target stock and short the acquirer's stock to lock in a hedge. Because there are two stocks involved in a stock-for-stock merger, the spread tends to fluctuate more than a cash merger spread does. This presents opportunity for the arbitrageur who is nimble enough to 'trade around the spread.'

Many arbs make a living by doing just that: buying spreads when they open and taking them off (selling the position) when they close. Trading prowess becomes more important for the arbitrageur in a stock for stock deal. As the two stocks involved in the deal fluctuate, an attractive spread may exist for only a brief moment. In that time, an arb must be successful in simultaneously buying the target stock and shorting the acquirer's stock at his desired prices. If he is off by even 1/8 of a dollar, it may lower the annualized return by several hundred basis points.

The need to be short the acquirer introduces some other elements into the arbitrage game. An arb must make sure that he can 'borrow' the stock he wants to short. In a short sale, the seller is selling stock that he does not own, but rather has borrowed. The arbitrageur's clearing house (brokerage firm) will lend him the stock if it can borrow it from another owner.

In addition to the issue of whether the stock is available to borrow, another problem with shorting arises should a deal break. Not only does the target stock fall, but the buyer's stock usually rises, causing losses for the arbs who have shorted the acquirer's stock. The acquirer's stock trades up because most of the arbitrage community is forced to cover the short and buy back the stock, creating upward pressure on its price, and losses for those that are short.

While stock-for-stock mergers are somewhat riskier for the arbitrageur, they often present very attractive spreads and returns. One such deal was the Gillette-Duracell merger in 1996.

Gillette Buys Duracell in Stock-for-Stock Merger

In September 1996, Gillette Co. announced that it would purchase battery maker Duracell International Inc. for $7.8 billion in stock and debt. Gillette would swap 0.904 of its shares for each Duracell share. Based on Gillette's closing share price of $66, the value of the bid was worth $59.66 per Duracell share, well above Duracell's price of $49.13.

Both stocks traded higher on the news because the merger made strategic sense. The purchase of Duracell would enhance Gillette's drive to become the leading consumer goods manufacturer. Duracell batteries would soon stand beside Gillette's other products such as Right Guard deodorants, Braun shavers, and Paper Mate pens, giving Gillette a larger share of the consumer products market. For Duracell, not only would the merger give its shareholders immediate price appreciation, but the company would benefit from Gillette's significant international presence and its promotion and distribution capabilities. The deal would increase both firms' revenue growth rates, create cost savings synergies, and be immediately accretive to earnings.

Gillette management was of the opinion that the market would react favorably to the acquisition and would likely bid up Gillette stock. This is one reason they had decided to do a stock deal, rather than pay in cash. The fact that Gillette stock had doubled in the past two years, combined with the stock's anticipated rise after the announcement, made Gillette stock a strong currency to use.

The arbitrageur's concern was not so much how profitable the merged entity would be going forward, but rather what return he would stand to make and the likelihood of deal consummation. Because Gillette did not currently manufacture batteries, regulatory concerns would not likely be an issue. As for the shareholder vote, Kohlberg Kravis Roberts held 45% of the outstanding Duracell shares. They had announced that they would vote in favor of the merger, assuring arbs that the shareholder vote would not impede the deal.

If the deal were likely to be consummated, what return did the arbitrageur stand to make? As mentioned, Gillette's current price of $66/share valued Duracell at $59.66/share. After the deal was announced, arbs bought Duracell stock at about $57.50 share. This created a spread (between $59.66 and $57.50) of approximately $2.16. If the arbs could simultaneously short 0.904 shares of Gillette at $66 and buy one share of Duracell at $57.50, he would lock in a profit of $2.16 per share. To explain how this is done, consider the following transaction in which an arbitrageur buys 1000 shares of Duracell and shorts 904 shares of Gillette to lock in the deal spread:

The Math

Initial Trade (September 12, 1996):

	Per Share	Per 1000 Shares
Buy 1000 Duracell shares at	$57.50	$57,500
Sell short 904 Gillette shares at	$66.00	$59,664
Duracell value ($66 * 0.904)	$59.66	$59,664
Spread ($59.66 - $57.50)	$2.16	$2,164
Return ($2.16/$57.50)	3.76%	3.76%
Holding period (typical stock deal)	3 months	3 months
Annualized return	15.04%	15.04%

Deal Closes 12/31/96:

Gillette closing price	$77.75
Per share loss on Gillette short (66 - 77.75)	-$11.75
Loss on Gillette position (904 * 11.75)	-$10,622
Value of Duracell share (77.75 * 0.904)	$70.29
Per share gain on Duracell (70.29 - 57.5)	$12.79
Gain on Duracell position (1000 * 12.79)	$12,790
Arbitrage profit (12,790 - 10,622)	$2,178
Initial investment (1000 * 57.50)	$57,500
Return to Arb (2,178/57,500)	3.76%

This was the actual profit that arbitrageurs made in the Gillette-Duracell deal. An important thing to note is that regardless of whether Gillette shares had gone up or down, an arbitrageur would have profited by locking in the $2.16 spread. Had Gillette fallen in value, the money would have been made mostly on the Gillette short position, rather than on the Duracell long position. Other considerations not included in this example, such as dividends received on Duracell and paid on the Gillette short, and interest received on the Gillette short, also play into the calculation of return. This example, though, effectively summarizes the profit an arbitrageur can make in a stock-for-stock merger.

◆ ◆ ◆

Chapter 7: Less Common Deals

The Statue of Zeus (433 BC).
The statue was 40 feet tall and a
symbol of perfection. Every year
thousands of ancient Greeks went
to pay homage to it.

Minority Buyouts

In this type of transaction, a majority shareholder makes an offer to purchase the minority stake of a company that it does not already own. For example, if a large corporation owns 75% of another (smaller) company, it may make a bid for the remaining 25% of the common stock that it does not already own. The 25% stake for which it bids is known as the 'minority ownership' of the smaller corporation. Those shareholders comprising the 25% are merged out, almost always at a premium, for their stock. The smaller company is then operated as a unit of the buyer going forward.

There are several reasons why a majority shareholder would do a minority buyout. After a buyout, management can implement strategic initiatives without the need to consider minority holders. The target becomes a private company, which frees up management time previously spent on public company policies like shareholder meetings. It also reduces the accounting, auditing, and earnings reporting costs that are associated with being public. In some cases, there are sizable tax benefits. In most cases, the buyer attempts to pay a less than economic price for the minority position.

Rhone-Poulenc SA Buys 32% of Rhone-Poulenc Rorer

On June 25, 1997, Rhone-Poulenc (RP) announced that it was considering buying the 32% stake of its U.S subsidiary, Rhone-Poulenc Rorer that it did not already own. RP wanted to increase its current 68% stake in the company to assume full ownership. In doing so, it would offer minority shareholders $92 per share in cash, which was a 16% premium to the previous day's closing price of $79.50.

The situation was as follows. RP was a major European producer of chemicals and pharmaceuticals, and Rorer was its U.S. pharmaceutical unit. RP management announced a restructuring in which it would spin off its chemical division, obtain 100% control of its U.S. pharmaceutical unit Rorer, and focus on its health care products going forward. This plan followed the industry trend of restructurings in chemicals and pharmaceuticals. This was a process of unwinding many of the conglomerates that were created in the 1960s and were not particularly successful.

When the news of the potential buyout was released on June 25, arbitrage buying pushed the stock price up to $91 per share. The arbitrageurs had several issues to consider. There was a standstill agreement in place that prevented RP from increasing its share in Rorer until July 31 of that year. Because of this, no deal could be made until August and timing became an issue. Also, an independent board was formed at Rorer to consider the bid, which many considered low. During July and much of August the special committee at Rorer negotiated but was unable to come to terms with RP, as the two sides were far apart on price. The arbitrageurs, meanwhile, continued to bid the stock up (over $95 per share) in anticipation of a higher bid from the parent. Finally, on August 20, Rorer announced that it had accepted a sweetened buyout bid from its parent company for $97 per share, and the deal closed soon thereafter. RP had successfully gained control of its U.S. subsidiary.

Overbids (The Plus – The Minus – But Mostly the Plus!)

Overbid situations are an arbitrageur's dream-come true. Sometimes, what started out as a peaceful merger or tender offer will erupt into a bidding war, with two or more potential acquirers competing for the target company. Such competition can yield excellent returns to the arbitrageur who is long the target stock. As each bid for the target stock is sequentially raised, the arb's returns are continually increased. In cash deals, higher bids are pure gravy on top of whatever return would have been earned otherwise.

One problem for the arbitrageurs in an overbid situation arises if the initial deal was to be a stock-for-stock transaction. For example, in the Gillette-Duracell deal, if another company had outbid Gillette, all of the arbitrageurs involved in the deal would have covered their Gillette shorts, forcing the stock up and creating losses for those that were short. They would have bought back their Gillette short because, if Gillette was no longer the buyer, there was no reason to be short the stock. These losses in Gillette may have partially offset their gains from a higher Duracell deal price.

Still, an arbitrageur will always want a higher bid to emerge for any stock that he is long. Such was the case in early 1996 when a bidding war erupted for cosmetics company Maybelline Inc.

Maybelline Inc. – The French Kiss

On December 10, 1995, French cosmetics giant L'Oreal S.A. and U.S. based Maybelline Inc. announced that they had reached a definitive merger agreement. L'Oreal would launch a cash tender offer of $36.75 per share for all of the 13.8 million Maybelline shares outstanding. After the announcement, arbs bought Maybelline stock in the open market at $36.25, anticipating that they would receive $36.75 for their shares in the cash tender.

An arb analyst who had carefully read the Schedule 14D-9 (merger document) filed by Maybelline would have known that during the negotiations between L'Oreal and Maybelline, a second bidder had emerged. Page 13 (lucky 13?) of the document explained that a second bidder had offered $36 per share, subject to completing its own corporate approval and due diligence. The Maybelline board decided, however, that given the two contingencies and the lower indicated bid price, it would accept L'Oreal's offer. But, having read this document, the arbitrageur would have quickly concluded that another buyer was lurking in the wings.

Sure enough, on January 15, 1996, one month after the L'Oreal-Maybelline merger announcement, the German consumer products maker Bensicker GmbH announced that it would outbid L'Oreal in its intended purchase of Maybelline. Bensicker told Maybelline that it would offer at least $37 a share and that it was prepared to pay a 'materially higher' price if certain conditions were met. Maybelline stock opened that day at $40 a share. The arbs were ecstatic. It looked as though a bidding war for the company was underway and the arbs who had bought Maybelline were along for the ride. The talk on the Street was that the final price of such a deal could be in the mid to high $40 per share range.

Just a few days later, on January 18, L'Oreal came back with an offer of $41 per share for Maybelline. In open market trading that day, arbs bid

Maybelline stock up to $42⅜ per share. They were certain that Bensicker would come back and top the $41 L'Oreal bid. The next day, Bensicker did tell Maybelline that it was prepared to top L'Oreal's sweetened bid, and Maybelline stock traded as high as $44⅞. This would turn out to be the top tick in the stock, though. On January 22, Maybelline agreed to a final L'Oreal offer of $44 a share. Bensicker said that it would not make a counteroffer and the bidding war was over. L'Oreal closed the tender on February 9 and the deal was complete at $44 per share.

Most of the arbitrageurs that were involved in this deal made a tremendous amount of money. Any arb who bought Maybelline in the low forties and below realized profits. Those few who got carried away in the euphoria and paid over $44 actually had small losses. But the arbitrageurs who had bought Maybelline on news of the initial deal profited the most. They earned a profit of $7.75 a share in just two months. Their return of 21% equated to an annualized return of 126%! Such are the rewards that are reaped in an overbid arbitrage deal. The kiss is sweet!

Leveraged Buyouts (LBO's)

As the name suggests, LBOs are transactions in which the buyer uses borrowed funds to make the acquisition. Generally, the acquiring entity takes out loans to pay for the acquisition and repays the loans over time with the cash flow of the target firm. At the time of the transaction, the target company's assets usually serve as collateral for the loans. Management will sometimes use this technique as a means of gaining control of its own company, taking the firm private. In other instances, an acquiring firm will use its own assets as collateral for the loans.

The funds are usually borrowed from a financial institution; most often from a bank, sometimes from an insurance company. Other times, the money is raised by issuing bonds that will be paid by the acquiring company. This was common in the 1980s, when corporate raiders issued low rated junk bonds to finance many of their acquisitions.

Purchases are done via an LBO for one of several reasons. If an acquirer does not have the requisite cash for the transaction on hand, it will consider an LBO. Similarly, if the acquiring firm does not want to dilute its own share base by paying in stock, it can make the purchase by doing an LBO. As long as the acquiring firm can borrow the funds at an acceptable rate, the LBO method is a rather cheap way of paying for a target company.

The primary concern for an arbitrageur in an LBO deal is that the financing is in place. The arb must make sure that the deal will not fall through due to a lack of financing and that the loans have been secured.

Stubs and Recapitalizations

Recapitalization is really just a fancy word for the alteration of a company's capital structure, such as an exchange of debt for equity. Any time a target firm is bought via an LBO, the firm will trade its equity in exchange for the assumption of some form of debt. In most cases, the buyer intends to take the target company private for some period of time, tune up the company in order to enhance its appeal to other buyers, and then sell it back to the public.

Often time, the buyer will leave a small stake in the company to trade publicly. The amount that is left public is usually 10% to 15% of the outstanding common stock. This 10-15% is known as the 'stub.' Why is this done? There are several reasons, but the most common deals with the concept of fresh start accounting. If the entire company is purchased the acquirer has to record 'goodwill' (the amount of the purchase price in excess of the company's assets) on its books. The amount of goodwill must eventually be written off, lowering reported earnings--and lowering the company's stock price. By leaving the 10-15% stub to trade publicly, an acquirer does not have to write off goodwill and take a hit to earnings.

Often, the best investment play here is for the arb to buy the stub. If the acquirer succeeds in boosting the target company's appeal, the stub may soar in price. Wealthy investors commonly commit to participate in LBO partnerships. Investors who buy the stubs ride along with the LBO pools--they're investing in the same companies--yet they don't have to pay the hefty management fees and they get liquidity to boot. Two such leveraged stubs were Thomas H. Lee's 1996 purchase of Syratech Corporation and KKR's 1997 purchase of the Amphenol Corporation.

Thomas H. Lee Fund Purchases Syratech Corporation

In October of 1996, giftware maker Syratech Corporation and the Thomas H. Lee Company, a private investment firm, announced that they had entered into an agreement in which Thomas Lee would purchase Syratech for $32 a share in cash. The acquisition would be funded with the assumption of up to $285 million of debt securities, consisting of a bond issuance and a senior revolving credit facility.

There were approximately 9 million shares of Syratech outstanding, which brought the total value of the offer to about $288 million. However, the merger agreement stipulated that 868,000 shares would remain outstanding, and not be purchased by Lee. This left the cash portion of the transaction at about $260 million (8.1 million shares * $32/share). The bulk of this price would be financed via the debt issuance described above.

The arbitrageurs' primary concern with the deal was whether the financing had been secured. Indeed, it had been. According to the merger document, Syratech had already obtained commitments for a planned $155 million debt issuance. Also, it had secured a $130 million revolving credit line with NationsBank, N.A. While the $155 million debt issuance would leave Syratech a highly leveraged entity (shareholders equity would be only $22 million going forward), the plan was feasible and the financing was in place. The major arbitrage concern in any LBO (financing) had been eased. Because most LBOs result in an extremely leveraged target company, Syratech was not an unusual case. On April 16, 1997, the deal closed and arbitrageurs were paid $32 a share in cash for the Syratech positions they had taken.

KKR's Purchase of the Amphenol Corporation and the Amphenol Stub

On January 23, 1997, Amphenol, a leading manufacturer of electrical equipment, announced that Kohlberg Kravis Roberts & Co. (KKR) would purchase it in a $1.05 billion merger. KKR was a private investment firm that had made a name for itself specializing in LBOs during the 1980s. For KKR, the merger represented an opportunity to participate in the upside prospects for Amphenol's earnings and cash flow going forward. For Amphenol, KKR would provide top line financial resources and expertise, enabling the company to pursue new product development, acquisitions, and investments. However, there was some question as to whether Amphenol shareholders were receiving a fair price and whether or not they should tender their shares.

The structure of the deal was such that KKR would purchase 90% of the Amphenol outstanding common stock for $26 a share, and leave the other 10% 'stub' public, to trade in the open market. Amphenol shareholders were given a choice of (a) receiving the $26 a share cash or (b) not tendering their shares, thus electing to retain part of the 10% stub that would continue to trade in the open market.

For those shareholders not tendering their shares, there was one issue: KKR would leave only 4.4 million (of the 46 million outstanding) to trade as the stub. Hence, if more than 4.4 million shares elected the stub, those shares would be pro-rated. For example, if 8.8 million shares elected to remain part of the stub, each person electing such option would only be allowed to retain half of his shares, and would receive $26 a share cash for the other half.

The decision facing the arbitrageur that played this deal was to tender or to choose the stub. After the announcement of the deal, Amphenol stock traded at about $25.50 a share. This left a tendering arb with a spread of only $0.50 ($26-$25.50), a return of 2%, or 6% annualized. The spread was small for a couple of reasons. First, the price appeared low. At $26, KKR was paying only 15x Amphenol's 1997 earnings, while its competitors traded at 17-18x earnings. Some analysts believed that another company might come in and pay over $30 a share, which would greatly enhance the return to the arbitrageur. The second reason for the low spread was that arbs could elect the stub. If Amphenol was cheap, even at $26 a share, many arbs thought that the play was to stay long the stub, participating with the savvy KKR on Amphenol upside. Either way, the downside was limited and the upside appeared substantial.

The merger was subject to certain conditions, including the completion of financing arrangements and Amphenol shareholder approval. Because the deal was in the form of a leveraged buyout, financing arrangements included the assumption of $750 million in loans and the issuance of $240 million in debt securities to fund the cash payment. As was the case with Syratech, Amphenol would be extremely leveraged following the transaction. The shareholder vote condition was satisfied in May of 1997, with a 79% majority voting in favor of the merger. The transaction closed a few days thereafter.

As was expected, more than the maximum number of 4.4 million shares held had elected the stub option. Approximately 9 million shares did not tender, choosing to remain part of the stub. They were pro-rated at about 50% and received $26 a share cash for the other 50%. As with many 'leveraged stub' deals, those shareholders electing the stub made the right decision. Within one year, Amphenol stock was trading at $61 a share in the open market! It had more than doubled in its first year as a stub.

From a return standpoint, any arbitrageur who had elected the stub had two returns. He received $26 a share cash in May 1997 for 50% of his stock. This was the forced acceptance of the cash portion because the stub was oversubscribed. The four-month return (based on buying at $25.50 and receiving $26) was 2%, or 6% annualized. However, if he held onto the stub, he realized a 139% one-year return on that portion of his investment. Combining the two, the Amphenol return to arbitrageurs was 72%. The power of the stub.

Liquidations

Liquidations are often classified as risk arbitrage plays as they are non-market correlated and require the analysis that is inherent in the arb process. Liquidations arise when a corporation decides that it will cease to operate and will sell, or liquidate, its assets. In general, a company will do this when it no longer elects to remain a going concern. These situations present an opportunity because such companies are often worth more in liquidation than they are as an ongoing entity. Make no mistake about it; this kind of investment is not a bet that a troubled company can turn itself around or begin generating earnings. Arb plays on liquidation are bets that the sum of the company's assets is more than the price at which its stock is currently trading.

Management Assistance Inc. - Long Drawn Out

In the increasingly competitive computer industry of the 1980s, a small-business computer maker called Management Assistance (MA) had gone from a 1979 profit of $19 million to a 1984 loss of $17 million. Asher Edelman, a corporate raider known for liquidating rather than running the companies he owned, obtained control of MA by use of a proxy fight. Just months after securing control, Edelman adopted a plan of liquidation for the company. It was agreed that MA would sell its two operating divisions, Basic Four and Sorbus Service, distribute the proceeds to shareholders, and then form a 'liquidating trust' to complete the distribution of any remaining assets.

After the sale of both divisions in January 1985, two distributions were made to shareholders. The first was a $7.85 debenture (bond) per share of common stock from the sale of its Basic Four Division. The second was a cash distribution of $18 per share. Soon thereafter, the remaining assets were transferred to the newly formed Management Assistance Liquidating Trust. MA common stock was then delisted from the New York Stock Exchange and shareholders received units in the trust in exchange for their shares.

The trust had been formed to liquidate any remaining non-cash assets and to handle the management of such assets until they were liquidated. The trust was a typical arbitrage liquidation play. The trust was originally to be dissolved in January 1989, but because of pending litigation and taxation issues affecting the company (and, as some have argued, reimbursement of the fees to the trustees), it remained in existence until January 1997.

As an example of how such a trust in liquidation continues to hold some value and presents an arbitrage opportunity, consider the December 31, 1995 balance sheet of the liquidating trust:

Assets (thousands of dollars)	
Cash and cash equivalents	$2,422
Tax refund receivable	148
Annuities	3,357
Total Assets	5,927
Liabilities	
Pension Liabilities	$3,357
Total Liabilities	3,357
Net Assets	$2,570

Liquidations are valued on a net asset basis. So, assuming that the net assets would be dispersed to the unit holders, based on 6,770,020 units outstanding, the value per unit was $0.38 (2.57 million / 6.77 million). At this time, the units traded in the open market at a price between $0.25 and $0.32, a discount to net asset value. Over the course of the next year, the liquidating trust was dissolved and holders were paid three different distributions: two payments of $0.25 each (relating to tax refunds the company received), and one final liquidating distribution, on January 9, 1997, $0.126 per unit. Hence, in the course of one year an arbitrageur who had purchased a unit at year-end 1995 at between $0.25 and $0.32, would have received total distributions of $0.626 per unit, a 100% return on his money.

◆ ◆ ◆

Chapter 8: The Cast

The Temple of Artemis (550 BC). King Croesus of Lydia built a magnificent temple to honor the goddess Artemis...it attracted worshippers from far and wide.

The arbitrageurs are just one group in the sea of participants in the mergers and acquisitions game. In their analysis of a deal, the arbs take into account the role of several other players that will have an effect on the outcome of any given merger. The group is a diverse assortment of professionals ranging from the investment bankers on center stage to the proxy solicitors who operate behind the scenes. This chapter will explain the roles that these groups take and the effect that each one has on the likelihood that a deal will be completed.

Wall Street Analysts

Wall Street equity analysts are a good source of information. These analysts generally spend their careers covering companies in only one industry and so they become experts in the field. Because an arbitrageur analyzes mergers across the broad spectrum of industries, they often need the specific industry expertise of an analyst. For example, an arbitrageur analyzing a potential merger between two auto parts companies may have no familiarity with the auto parts industry, but he can gain valuable insight into it by speaking with an analyst who has spent his life following such firms. Even if the analyst is unavailable, an arbitrageur can usually retrieve the analyst's research reports on Wall Street data systems like First Call and Multex.

Many sell side analysts have excellent relationships with the managements of the companies they follow. This too can prove valuable to an arbitrageur, who can gain intuition from analysts on how management has reacted in previous deal scenarios and what they are likely to do in a current merger situation.

Arbitrageurs understand that analysts who work for the investment banks that are involved in transactions can be biased in their opinions. Often these analysts speak favorably about their clients (the companies they analyze) so that their firms retain the lucrative investment banking fees that are earned from such clients. Overall, the analysts' input is an important tool that, when used correctly, can yield timely and valuable information to the arbitrageur.

Institutional Shareholders

Institutional shareholders own 65% of the typical public equity traded in the United States. Because they account for such a large percent, they are often the swing factor in a merger vote. The largest groups of institutional shareholders include public-employee pension funds, corporate pension funds, and mutual funds.

Mutual fund managers control an increasing share of corporate equity in the U.S. As with public pensions, mutual funds are primarily concerned with annual returns and will most often vote or tender shares in favor of a merger that enhances shareholder value. However, depending on the fund manager's style, he or she can fall anywhere on the spectrum of shareholder activism. Beyond their concern for annual returns, some mutual fund managers have relationships with corporate management that they might not betray in a hostile deal.

Investment Bankers

The investment bankers are usually the creators and the facilitators of a deal. They are paid large fees by institutional clients for their merger and acquisition advice and expertise. Even if a merger is not the result of an investment banker's idea, he or she will likely have played a large role in the events leading up to the announcement of the deal. However, because these bankers are bound to secrecy regarding all aspects of the deal, it is hopefully rare that an arbitrageur will obtain information from the banker that is working on the deal.

In most merger documents, the investment bank representing each company involved in the merger will give its 'fairness opinion' as to whether the price at which the target company is being sold is adequate.

While these opinions can be biased in favor of the bank's client, they are a good reference point from which the arbitrageur can begin his analysis of the deal. The opinion usually states how the deal is priced relative to similar recent transactions in the same industry. This information helps the arbitrageur in deciding whether there is room for a higher bid or if it is already a richly priced transaction.

While an arbitrageur may not be able to talk to the investment banker working on a deal, he may speak to other investment bankers. Because these bankers specialize in merger and acquisition activity, they often know more about the business than anyone. Given their experience, even if they are not involved in a deal, they can provide an arbitrageur with valuable insight into potential pitfalls and past examples of M&A activity.

Lawyers – Whose Bread I Eat, His Song I Sing

Lawyers often play a role in the outcome of a merger transaction. Their legal role changes depending on whether the deal is friendly or hostile. In a friendly deal, lawyers serve two purposes. They advise on the contractual negotiations between the two merging entities, including the terms and structure of the deal, and they handle any other legal issues relating to the merger for their clients.

In a hostile deal, lawyers advise their clients on the legal aspects of takeover tactics. A hostile buyer can use his lawyers to ascertain the most effective method in which to proceed from a legal perspective. Target management, on the other hand, utilizes legal advice regarding the form of takeover defense it will adopt. In one instance, a target company may file several lawsuits against the bidder in an effort to rebuff the potential buyer or to stall for time and solicit a higher bid. Other times, a target company will simply use its lawyers to advise it on all possible legal outcomes regarding the impending hostile bid.

Several prominent corporate law firms dominate the field of mergers and acquisitions. Two of today's best known M&A law firms are Skadden, Arps, Slate, Meagher & Flom and Wachtell, Lipton, Rosen & Katz. Skadden rose to prominence in the late 1960s after the passage of the Williams Act. This act, which was designed to regulate tender offers, gave takeover lawyers like Skadden and others rules to interpret and a business in which to operate. While Skadden made a name for itself largely by representing hostile acquirers, Wachtell came to be known as the premier takeover-defense legal firm. In

1982, Marty Lipton developed and subsequently evolved the hideous (to shareholders) but well-known poison pill defense.

Due to their prominent role in merger and acquisition legal advice, antitrust lawyers are often sought after by risk arbitrageurs. Arbitrageurs generally have either in-house counsel that advises them on deals or they will pay a retainer to an outside M&A law firm for legal advice. The area in which lawyers are usually most helpful to the arbitrageurs is in ascertaining the probability of whether or not a deal will be blocked due to antitrust concerns. Lawyers can also advise an arbitrageur on a particular state's anti-takeover statutes and the legal effectiveness that a target's defense will have in staving off a hostile bid.

Proxy Solicitors

A proxy fight is a technique used by an acquiring company to try to gain control of its takeover target. The acquirer attempts to convince the shareholders of the target company that they should vote to remove the current management and replace them with a slate of directors chosen by the acquirer. If the shareholders cast their proxy votes in favor of the hostile acquirer, the acquirer has essentially obtained control of the target firm.

A proxy solicitor specializes in lobbying shareholders. Solicitors can be hired by any party involved in the proxy fight and are responsible for getting that group's message out to the shareholders and soliciting those shareholders' votes in their favor. Two of today's biggest firms are D.F. King & Company and Georgeson & Company. Their primary responsibility in a proxy fight is to conduct mass mailings and telephone calling in an effort to reach the target's shareholders.

The proxy solicitor can swing the proxy vote in favor of or against incumbent management. And because the proxy fight may often lay the groundwork for an eventual takeover of the target firm, the solicitors have an indirect effect on the likelihood of an eventual merger. If the arbitrageur has made a bet that a company will in fact be taken over, the proxy solicitor acting on behalf of a hostile acquirer becomes an ally to the arbitrageur.

The Press

The financial press has played an increasingly important role in the information available on merger and acquisition activity. Such reporting can have an altering effect on the manner in which different parties involved in such transactions view a merger.

Arbitrageurs usually make their initial investment decision before reading the merger document or speaking with the parties involved in the deal. Immediately after a deal is announced, press reports are often the only means of attaining preliminary information on the potential merger. Because the arbitrageur's investment in this situation is so dependent on the press reports, he must be extremely astute in deciphering fact from opinion and relevant data from immaterial information.

Three mediums of financial press have developed in recent times. The first is the traditional written press. The Wall Street Journal remains a leading source of merger and acquisition news. Managements understand the need and importance of managing the news. What better way to do it than to selectively leak information. The Journal is so adept at obtaining such information that many deals will be announced and written about on its front page before the deal has even been announced by the combining firms.

The second and increasingly important medium is television. CNBC has come to dominate this mode, and its programs appear continually on the television screens of major trading floors, hedge funds, and risk arbitrage operations. CNBC, along with competitors like CNNfn, not only report merger news but also editorialize it. The spin they put on stories has an impact on both Wall Street players and the millions of individual investors who watch the programs and then vote their shares in favor of or against a merger.

The third way merger and acquisition news is reported is through the newswires of Reuters, Dow Jones, and Bloomberg. All traders and arbitrageurs have scrolling headlines that appear on their quote terminals. These headlines are often the first to break deal news during the business day and have the first-story impact that can shape the perception of a deal.

The Lenders

The financiers of a deal are the commercial banks, the investment banks, and other financial intermediaries that provide the acquirer with the cash needed to finance its payment to the target shareholders. The cash is usually in the form of a bank loan, a bridge loan, or high yield debt.

Bank loans are long term loans from a bank to a corporate acquirer and are the most common source of funding for a cash deal. They are provided by large commercial banks like Chase or Citigroup and usually carry a floating rate (often LIBOR) plus a predetermined amount. The banks providing such loans are critical for the completion of a cash merger and whenever possible the arbitrageur must ascertain that these loans have been secured ahead of time.

Bridge loans are a more expensive, shorter-term form of financing. When using a bridge loan, an acquirer will pay a bank or other financial intermediary a high rate on a short term loan that is meant only to fill the gap until more permanent financing is obtained. The mere existence of a bridge loan in a deal will alert the arbitrageur to the possibility that financing has been and will be an issue in the final consummation of the deal. However, without the provision of bridge loans by certain financiers, many mergers would never even reach the announcement of the deal stage.

A third option for raising cash is for an acquirer to issue high yield debt. As discussed in Chapter 3, this became the preferred method of payment for hostile raiders in the 1980s. The facilitator of high yield debt financing is usually the investment bank that underwrites the bonds. Before the debt is placed, the bank issues what is known as a 'highly confident' letter, giving the market a degree of assurance that the funding will come through. While arbitrageurs will look to a highly confident letter for assurance, a bank loan commitment, a bridge loan, or the completion of the high yield issuance offer greater assurance.

The Regulators

> *"No corporation...shall acquire...the whole or any part of the stock...of another corporation...where in any line of commerce in any section of the country the effect of such acquisition may be substantially to lessen competition, or to tend to create a monopoly."*[9]

The two enforcers of such mandates as the one above are the Federal Trade Commission (FTC) and the Department of Justice (DOJ). These two entities generally have more influence over the eventual outcome of a merger than any of the other parties discussed in this chapter.

The FTC is comprised of hearing examiners and commissioners who specialize in a particular trade regulation field. The merger review process begins when the FTC examiner and his staff review the proposed transaction and its likely repercussions. The examiner then presents his conclusions to the FTC commission. The commission, in turn, votes on whether or not to approve a deal, to request additional information on the deal, or to block it on antitrust grounds.

FTC approval of the deal signifies to the arbitrageur that there are no antitrust concerns (this is what an arb wants to hear!). An FTC request for additional information means that there may be some antitrust issues, but they are probably resolvable. However, the merging companies will need more time to present the FTC with the new information and the merger will likely close at a later date than was originally anticipated. A blocking of the deal by the FTC means that the arbitrageurs are pretty much out of luck, and the two firms will not merge (as with Staples and Office Depot). The decision of the commission can be appealed in federal circuit courts but is rarely overturned.

The Antitrust Division of the Justice Department is the other regulatory agency that reviews and rules upon the anticompetitive nature of merger transactions. In contrast to the FTC, the Justice Department carries its proceedings through the federal court system.

As was discussed in Chapter 4, in addition to the FTC and DOJ, certain mergers may need approval from their respective industry regulatory boards. For example, the comptroller of the currency, the Federal Deposit Insurance Corporation, and the Federal Reserve are all active in the regulation of bank mergers. Deals in the railroad industry are subject to the approval of an agency known as the Surface Transportation Board. The Federal Communications Commission (FCC) must approve most mergers in the cable and telecommunication businesses. Finally, utility mergers can often take over a year to complete as they are subject to approval by both the Federal Energy Regulatory Commission (FERC) and numerous other state regulatory boards.

The Securities and Exchange Commission implements and enforces the laws and rules that govern merger procedure. The SEC requires that any acquirer launching a tender offer for another company file a Schedule 14D-1, and that any company involved in a merger (as opposed to a tender) file a proxy statement. These are known to arbitrageurs as the 'merger documents' and contain information that is extremely helpful in the analysis of a deal. Their contents include information like the background of events leading up to the tender offer, the nature of the funds being used, and the contingencies upon which the offer is based. The SEC's enforcement of such rules as the 14D-1 and proxy statement filings has greatly facilitated the job of the arbitrageur.

The Target Company and the Board

The board of directors and incumbent management have a big effect on when, how, and to whom their company will be sold. Because of this, the arbitrageur must know where they stand and how they are likely to react. Friendly deals, in which target management has agreed to merge with an acquirer, are more likely to be completed than hostile ones. The example of Lloyd Cotsen at Neutrogena (Chapter 5) is a classic example of a friendly seller facilitating the consummation of a deal.

Hostile deals, in which no firm agreement is in place, face numerous obstacles on their way to consummation. The hurdles they face include the many defense tactics that are employed by the board at target companies. These tactics will be discussed in greater detail in Chapter 10.

◆ ◆ ◆

Chapter 9: Offensive Strategies

The Mausoleum at Halicarnassus (4th Century BC). The magnificent tomb of King Mausolus of Caria was called a mausoleum, after his name.

There are many ways a potential acquirer can go about trying to purchase a target company. The most common procedure is for the buyer to contact the seller and negotiate an agreed upon amount that it will pay the shareholders of the target company. This process often works and many deals originate in such a manner. However, when the approached target is not receptive, an acquirer must resort to other means.

Bear Hugs

One method of trying to put into play a company that won't negotiate is the bear hug. In a bear hug, a prospective buyer makes a formal acquisition proposal to the board of directors of a target company. The offer is usually made in a letter to the board that appeals to the board's fiduciary responsibility to its shareholders. It pressures incumbent management to sell or in some way unlock the value in its shares. The actual term 'bear hug' comes from the fact that the pressure on target management is akin to the feeling one experiences when hugged by a bear.

When a buyer just wants to bring the target company to the negotiating table, the bear hug can be a 'soft' one, kept private between the two firms. This was the case with ITT Industries' bid for Goulds Pumps in 1997 (Chapter 6). ITT had been frustrated at Goulds' unwillingness to negotiate a friendly deal. Hence, in order to bring Goulds to the bargaining table, ITT made a 'soft' bear hug offer for the company. The offer was not announced publicly, but it privately forced Goulds to negotiate a deal.

Other times, when the buyer wants to put a company in play and activate the company's shareholders to force a sale, the buyer will go public with the bear hug. In this scenario, the bear hug is commonly the first step in the process of making a hostile bid for the target. The buyer's hope is that the pressure from shareholders and arbitrageurs who buy the stock after the announcement will eventually wear down a board of directors.

A bear hug is most effective when the target company has limited defenses and resources with which to stave off an interested acquirer. According to Eric Longmire, director of research at the arbitrage firm Wyser-Pratte & Co., there are "companies that want to do hostiles, but don't want to go the full way. These bear-hug letters are trying to get the shareholders to do the work."[10]

The true mettle of an arbitrageur is tested in a bear hug scenario. It is often difficult to ascertain what the eventual outcome of such an event will be. There exists a risk/return tradeoff between the hope of a bidding war and the possibility of a failure to complete any deal at all. The arbitrageur must do an initially cursory, and later more detailed, analysis of the firms involved. The arb considers the fundamental value of the target firm, the price of the bid, and the extent to which he thinks the offer can be raised. He also assesses the defenses that the target's board has put in place. The existence of poison pills and staggered boards can make it extremely difficult for a buyer to force a deal. Other times, a buyer can force a deal with an effective bear hug. Such was the case between American Home Products and American Cyanamid.

The American Bear Hug: Home Products and Cyanamid

In August 1994, American Home Products Chairman John Stafford launched a bear hug offer for his pharmaceutical rival, American Cyanamid. The activity of the firms preceding the offer had a lot to do with the way Home Products approached its target.

Stafford had been contemplating a merger with Cyanamid for several months. A purchase of Cyanamid would provide a much needed boost to Home Products' overall product portfolio. Stafford had even met informally with Cyanamid management and had set up a meeting for late August at which he planned to make a formal proposal to purchase Cyanamid. Before that meeting took place, though, market rumors began to leak out that Cyanamid was in talks with SmithKline Beecham regarding a swap of assets between the two companies. The speculation was that SmithKline would give Cyanamid its animal-health business in exchange for Cyanamid's prescription drug and consumer brands divisions. Because these divisions were the two that Stafford coveted most, he had to act quickly to break up a potential SmithKline-Cyanamid deal and buy Cyanamid for his own.

His decision was to launch a bear hug offer for Cyanamid for $8.5 billion, or $95 a share on August 3. This was a two-pronged plan of attack. The first prong was the decision to launch a bear hug without the inclusion of an official tender offer. There was no tender because Stafford was using the bear hug as a tool to bring Cyanamid to the bargaining table. A tenderless bear hug was a soft way of telling Cyanamid that it was going to be bought, but that Home Products would like to do so on a friendly basis.

The second prong to the attack was the fact that the $95 a share preemptive bid was very rich at about 21x Cyanamid's 1998 estimated earnings. $95 was a 50% premium to Cyanamid's stock price before the bid. Stafford's decision to offer such a high price was a concerted effort to stave off any other potential bidders. Although it would be an expensive acquisition, Stafford was betting that his strategy would both bring Cyanamid to the table and prevent a bidding war among several potential suitors.

Stafford's initial approach did not appear to be working, as Cyanamid did not respond within a week's time of the Home Products bid. Stepping up the intensity of the attack, Stafford launched a formal tender offer on August 10 and also sought a shareholder vote to remove Cyanamid's takeover defenses. Meanwhile, the arbitrageurs were paying only $93.50 a share for Cyanamid stock in the open market, indicating that they thought a second bidder was unlikely.

Unbeknownst to the arbitrageurs, Stafford's pressure had forced Cyanamid to the negotiating table with Home Products. In an unusual move, after just one day of negotiations with Cyanamid, Home Products upped its public offer to $100 a share. The bid was made to pressure Cyanamid into a quick response. It was made on the eve of Cyanamid's board meeting and Cyanamid was given only 24 hours to respond. Stafford was playing hardball. The move paid off when only one day later the two companies announced a friendly merger agreement of $101 a share.

American Home Products had adroitly obtained control of American Cyanamid. Beginning with a soft bear hug, the offer had turned into a hostile tender, forcing Cyanamid to negotiate a deal. Home Products' tactics worked. The deal illustrated the importance for arbitrageurs to know the options available to a hostile bidder and the approach that bidder is likely to take. Those arbs that were able to correctly assess the situation profited generously from the final price of the Cyanamid-Home Products deal.

Proxy Battles

Proxy fights can be an extremely effective weapon in helping a hostile acquirer attain control of its target company. A proxy battle is a direct attack on the corporate board of the target, as the would-be acquirer attempts to remove the incumbent slate of directors by way of a shareholder vote. For the acquirer, one advantage of waging a proxy battle is that it is a relatively cheap way for it to attain control of the target. If the shareholders vote in favor of replacing the incumbent board with a slate of directors proposed by the acquirer, the acquirer essentially gains control of the target. It has done so without spending the capital involved in an outright acquisition.

The threat of proxy battles can be used to weaken the defenses of a target company. Defense mechanisms like poison pills and staggered boards can be extremely difficult for the buyer to circumvent and will often prevent a hostile deal from ever being consummated. However, if the acquirer launches a proxy fight and successfully obtains control of the target board, it can then loosen the target's defense mechanisms that are keeping the deal from going through.

Because of their impact on the outcome of hostile deals, proxy battles are an important aspect of merger arbitrage analysis. Arbitrageurs will go to great lengths in determining the effect that a proxy fight will have on the result of an impending takeover battle. One deal in which the proxy analysis played a big role was in the hostile bid that IBM launched for Lotus Development Corp. in 1995.

IBM Goes Hostile

On June 5, 1995, IBM launched a bear hug cash tender offer of $60 a share for all the outstanding shares of Lotus Development, a desktop software manufacturer. After several attempts at negotiating a friendly transaction, IBM had been forced to turn hostile. Commenting on the strategy, IBM's general counsel Lawrence Ricciardi explained, "We had had conversations with Lotus and weren't able to persuade them to make a deal with us. We were concerned that if we kept pushing them on a friendly basis, we might drive them into the arms of a third party."[11] This situation was typical of many such instances that often resulted in a bear hug by a frustrated would be acquirer.

IBM's bid of $60 a share was nearly a 100% premium to the previous day's closing price of $32½. As with Home Products, the bid was purposely high so that other potential acquirers would not be drawn into the fight and that the transaction could close sooner. IBM did not want to lose what was Lotus's greatest asset – its employees. A quick strike at a high price would hopefully accelerate the process.

The hostile bid was only the first part of IBM's strategy. Along with the offer, IBM announced that it would commence a proxy fight in an effort to oust the board at Lotus. The reason for this was that Lotus had a poison pill, or shareholder's rights plan, which would have made an acquisition of the firm prohibitively expensive. If IBM could replace the Lotus board and insert its own slate of directors, IBM would be able to remove the poison pill and proceed with its takeover. What facilitated the proxy process for IBM was that the Lotus by-laws allowed an insurgent to solicit shareholder votes regarding the replacement of the board at any time, without having to wait for the annual shareholder meeting. If it was successful in its proxy, IBM could effectively replace the entire board within two months.

The strategy implemented by IBM had been well thought out and would be difficult to fight. Realizing this, Lotus came to the bargaining table to negotiate an agreement with IBM. After several days of discussion, IBM agreed to pay $64 a share in a friendly deal for Lotus. By combining a bear hug with a proxy threat, IBM had effectively consummated a transaction that had stalled under the original friendly overture.

Hostile Tenders – The "Grizzly Bear"

A hostile tender offer is the most aggressive form of bear hug and has become the weapon of choice in waging a takeover battle. One of the earliest forms of tenders, known as the Saturday Night Special, became a successful takeover strategy in the 1970s. At the time, the SEC required that a tender offer be outstanding for only seven calendar days. This gave the target limited time in which to organize its defensive strategy.

Capitalizing on this, buyers began launching bids on Saturday afternoon of the weekend, giving the target even less time to respond.

Later in the 70s, the required length of a tender was lengthened to twenty days, reducing the effectiveness of the Saturday Night Special. But the hostile tender was still the most effective means of waging a takeover campaign and was widely used by the hostile raiders of the 1980s. In the 1990s, hostile tenders have become more difficult to effect because of improved anti-takeover defenses and a legal climate that has increasingly favored target companies. However, they are still the preferred means of initiating a hostile acquisition.

When a hostile tender is announced for a target, the target stock usually trades at a slight premium to the tender price. The arbs pay this premium based on the assumption that either the acquirer will raise its bid, or the target will find another buyer who is willing to pay more. But because the final result and expected return are unknown, the arbitrage research is a less exact, but equally grueling art form.

A 1997 study conducted by J.P. Morgan identified the end result of 74 hostile takeover attempts. There were three scenarios: 36% of the time, the target was sold to the hostile bidder; 30% of the time the target company was acquired by another suitor; and only 34% of the time did the target company remain independent. This meant that 66% of all hostile offers resulted in some form of transaction. Arbitrage analysis in a hostile deal involves understanding these probabilities and the extent to which they change in different circumstances.

One way in which a potential acquirer tries to enhance its chances is by buying shares of the target company. In this case, a would be acquirer begins buying the target stock, accumulating a position of 5% or more before it launches the tender offer. Owning the target stock has several benefits to the acquirer. First, it shows that the acquirer really does think the target stock is undervalued and is very serious about buying the company. Second, stock ownership gives the buyer voting power in any shareholder vote that might affect the outcome of a merger. Finally, if another suitor outbids the acquirer, the acquirer will at least have a gain in the stock it bought prior to putting the target in play, thereby offsetting the costs it incurred in the process.

◆ ◆ ◆

Chapter 10: Playing Defense

*The Colossus of Rhodes (300 BC).
The people of Rhodes built an enormous
statue of Helios, to thank their god for
protecting them. It towered to a height
of 120 feet, more than 20 times life size.*

Target management that is determined to prevent a takeover is usually the biggest impediment that prevents a hostile deal from being completed. There are many forms of defense that a company can take to ward off a hostile bidder, from selling off assets to altering the structure of its board. A risk arbitrageur must be cognizant of the various defenses available to a firm and the effectiveness with which the various techniques will work in different circumstances. Dissection of a target's defense mechanisms is the cornerstone of 'hostile deal' risk arbitrage analysis.

Any defense is most effective when put into place before a combatant has reached the battlefield. For this reason, anticipatory defenses are usually put in place long before a hostile suitor approaches a company. The best defense is a company management that enhances shareholder value by growing the business and increasing the stock price. Other anticipatory defenses include the adoption of a poison pill, a staggered board, and other measures known as shark repellents. Once the hostile bid has been launched, an unwilling seller can use additional techniques like negotiating a standstill agreement or finding a white knight. This chapter will discuss pre-bid defenses and post-bid defenses and the use of each in the Pennzoil and ITT hostile takeover attempts.

Anticipatory Defenses

Poison Pill

Shareholder rights plans, commonly known as poison pills, have become the takeover prevention method of choice in corporate America. Their origin is attributed to takeover defense lawyer Marty Lipton who developed the first poison pill in 1982. In 1985, the Delaware Supreme Court legitimized the concept by ruling that the board of a corporation could issue a poison pill as a preventive takeover measure. After this, a bevy of companies adopted the measure, seeking to protect themselves from the hostile raiders of the 1980s. Today, more than two thirds of the companies in the S&P 500 index have rights plans known as poison pills. Regrettably, few managements have given shareholders the option of voting on these pills.

The pill is relatively simple to put in place. To implement it, a company issues to existing shareholders one stock purchase right for every share each stockholder currently owns. Each right gives the shareholder the option to purchase one share at a steep discount to the prevailing market price. The trick is that the right is not triggered until one shareholder owns more than a certain percent of the company (usually 20%). If such a shareholder (in theory a hostile acquirer) breaks the ownership percent threshold, every stockholder except the one exceeding the ownership limit is entitled to exercise his right and buy a discounted share. When this is done, the value of the large shareholder's stake is greatly reduced and his ownership in the target is diluted.

The poison pill is put in place by the board of directors and is usually in effect for a period of ten years. It is rare that the pill will ever be activated, but rather it serves as a deterrent against an unwanted buyer. When a hostile bidder does come, the existence of a pill forces the buyer to negotiate with the board of the company, since only the board can remove the pill. The pill also gives management of the target the time to organize its defenses before the buyer can acquire a substantial position in its stock. Many shareholders view the pill as an example of shareholder disenfranchisement. Others view it as a form of management entrenchment. We view it from the eyes of an arb.

Poison Pill Example

Park Autos, Inc.:	100 shares outstanding
	$1 per share
	Company market value = $100
	Poison pill is triggered at above 20% ownership by any one holder
Hostile Buyer:	Takes a 25% position in Park – buys 25 shares (triggers poison pill)
	Stake worth $25
Other shareholders:	Initially have a $75 stake
	Then, exercise their poison pill buy right – buy 75 shares
	Now 75 new shares outstanding – total 175 shares outstanding.
Post-rights exercise:	Company market value still = $100
	New price per share = $0.57 = $100 value / 175 shares
Result:	Because Hostile Buyer did not get any new shares, the value of its stake is significantly reduced. It is now worth only $14.28 (=25 shares * $0.57 per share), down from $25.
	The loss that Hostile Buyer would incur as a result of the poison pill will deter it from attempting to acquire a large stake in the company.

One problem with the poison pill defense is that a hostile acquirer can launch a bid for a company contingent upon the removal of the poison pill. To ensure removal, the acquirer will then attempt to oust the existing directors, and replace them with a board that will eliminate the poison pill. In response to such measures, companies began to adopt 'Dead Hand' poison pills. The dead hand pill gives only the incumbent board of directors the right of pill removal. Hence, even if the acquirer forces out the incumbent directors, the new board cannot remove the poison pill. While dead hands are rare, it is important for the arbitrageur to know if the target's rights plan is a dead hand, standard, or other form of pill.

Staggered Board

The stamina of the board of directors is essential to the target company's ability to fend off a hostile acquirer. One way that a company ensures that its board will not be quickly replaced by a hostile proxy fight is to structure the board in a staggered form. To do so, the company amends its charter so that only a certain number of its directors come up for re-election each year. The board is usually divided into three classes, with each class coming up for re-election in a different year. In this manner, a hostile acquirer can replace only one third of the directors each year, taking it at least two years to assume control of the board. The existence of a staggered board and a poison pill in tandem make it extremely difficult for a hostile acquirer to effect a takeover.

In addition to staggering the re-election of board members, there are other steps a company can take to solidify the position of the incumbent directors. One measure is for the company to require a supermajority vote (of, for example, 90%) to remove a director from the board. It is very difficult for an insurgent shareholder to obtain such a high percent of the vote in favor of its directive to remove a board member. Similarly, a company can implement charter bylaws that limit the size of the board to its current number of directors. This move was introduced to combat raiders who tried to keep adding their own new members to the board until they had control.

The important issue for the arbitrageur is to understand the structure of the board and the ease or difficulty with which it can be replaced by an acquirer. This is often dependent upon the laws of the state in which the company is incorporated. In general, the stronger the incumbent board and the more defenses it has built, the less likely it is that a hostile offer will result in a merger transaction and profits for the arbitrageur.

Other Shark Repellents

The supermajority mandate can also be applied to the shareholder vote for an actual merger. Some companies' charters will state that any merger that the firm enters into requires a supermajority approval of 90%. It is near impossible for a hostile acquirer to obtain a 90% vote in favor of its merger offer. In fact, many companies do not use this defense because it can even make the approval for a friendly deal difficult to obtain.

Large compensation payments to management of the target, known as golden parachutes, are another form of defense that a company can install before it becomes the target of an aggressor. Silver and platinum parachutes work in a similar manner, except that they guarantee either compensation or continued benefits for many employees in the event the employee leaves the firm because of a merger. Sometimes golden parachutes are not implemented as a defense mechanism, but rather as a result of management's own self-interest to receive extra compensation.

Nevertheless, they can make an unsolicited takeover offer extremely expensive for the acquirer.

Pennzoil Fights Off UPR – Just Say No

In June 1997, Union Pacific Resources launched a $4 billion hostile tender offer for rival oil exploration and production firm Pennzoil Co. Pennzoil's ensuing defense was a classic example of how management with built-in defenses can 'just say no.' The UPR all-cash offer was for $84 a share, a 41% premium to Pennzoil's previous close of $59. Arbitrageurs bid Pennzoil stock up into the mid $70 a share range, anticipating that a deal in some form would eventually be completed.

They had not fully taken into account the numerous defenses that the company had. First and foremost, Pennzoil had a poison pill in place. This hindrance could only be removed by the company's board of directors and the board of directors was not leaving any time soon. The board was staggered so that only one third of its members were up for re-election each year. This meant that it would take a minimum of two years for UPR to gain control of the board and remove the poison pill. Furthermore, the Pennzoil board had implemented a by-law that prohibited its shareholders from calling a special meeting to oust the company's directors. With a poison pill in place and a board of directors that was entrenched for at least two years, it was unlikely that any outsider could force a sale of the company.

A month after the initial bid, 61.5% of Pennzoil shareholders tendered their stock in favor of the UPR bid. However, because of the rigid poison pill that was in place, UPR could not acquire those shares. Pennzoil management stubbornly continued to argue that it could enhance shareholder value on its own and wanted to remain independent. After considering the legal expenses and other costs involved in pursuing such a bid, UPR announced in November that it would pull its offer if Pennzoil would not negotiate a deal. On the announcement, Pennzoil stock plunged $9 from $74 to $65 a share, causing loss and pain for the arbitrageurs still involved in the deal. True to its word, UPR pulled its bid in late November.

Arbitrageurs sold their Pennzoil holdings at losses of between $10-15 a share, depending on where they had bought the stock. In the next year, Pennzoil would trade down to below $30 a share. Clearly, its management had been incorrect in its prediction of being able to enhance shareholder value on its own. But it did not matter. When the defenses are as solidly in place as they were at Pennzoil, there is little opportunity for the consummation of a hostile deal and arbitrage profits.

Post-Bid Defenses

The aforementioned defenses are all ways in which a potential target prepares for the possibility of a hostile bid. Those defenses are put in place before a bid actually occurs. Once a hostile offer does come, the real game of defense begins. Some of the most common ways to play that game are discussed below.

Standstill Agreement

One approach for the already in-play target to take is to ask the potential acquirer to sign a standstill agreement. The standstill is a contract signed by both the acquirer and the target, in which neither party can pursue an acquisition with the other unless it is done on friendly terms. It benefits the target company in that the agreement enables it to negotiate a deal without the threat of the buyer going hostile. That is, any final agreement will be in accordance with the interests of the target. The reason that an acquirer would be willing to sign a standstill is that it brings the target to the negotiating table. Because it is quite likely that an agreement will be reached once a standstill is signed, the acquirer attains his ultimate goal of consummating the transaction.

Pac Man Defense

In the game Pac Man, the *chasee* becomes the *chaser* after ingesting a special kind of potion. In a similar way, a target company becomes an acquirer when it employs what is known as the Pac Man defense. When this happens, a company that has received a hostile takeover bid from an unwanted solicitor counters with a bid for the solicitor itself.

For example, in 1981, Martin Marietta responded to a rival bid from competitor Bendix Corp. by turning around and making an offer to buy Bendix. The tactic eventually succeeded by forcing the original bidder, Bendix, to be acquired by AlliedSignal Corp.

More than anything else, the Pac Man defense causes confusion and uncertainty for the arbitrageur and other investors. It is sometimes employed as a means of giving the original target more time to prepare its defenses. Other times, the original target believes that a merger does make strategic sense, but that its management should be the one to run the combined entity. Many times, the first tender launched will be the only successful one because of its first mover advantage in obtaining control of the other corporation. For an arbitrageur to profit in these situations, it is critical that he understands the tender offer rules and historical precedents.

Greenmail

The term greenmail refers to a target company's voluntary repurchase of a hostile would-be acquirer's shares. If the target pays the acquirer a large enough premium for its stock in the target, the acquirer is often willing to walk away from a hostile takeover battle. For example, in 1985, T. Boone Pickens had amassed a stake in oil company Phillips Petroleum before launching a hostile offer for Philips. In order to avert a takeover battle and remain independent, Phillips paid T. Boone $53 a share ($10 over the market price) for the Phillips stock he owned. Content with his profit, Pickens no longer pursued his bid for Phillips and walked away. Because it is a form of blackmail and involves the payment of large sums of money, this practice has come to be known as 'greenmail'.

Selling the Crown Jewel

Another alternative is for the target company to sell off certain assets or units of the company. The idea with this defense is to make the target less attractive to the hostile acquirer. Sometimes an acquirer will launch a bid for a company because it covets one particular asset or division. If that asset is sold or spun-off, the buyer might lose interest in the target and the target will remain independent.

Although this strategy usually thwarts the completion of a deal, it can be advantageous even for the arbitrageur. This is because the true value of the company is realized through the sale of the asset. The sale of an undervalued asset serves as a catalyst to unlock the hidden value of the target company. As such, the target stock that the arbitrageur owns can trade higher even without the completion of a merger.

Self-Tender

Sometimes, a target company will launch a self-tender for a portion of its own shares, at a premium to the price being offered by the hostile acquirer. As a stand-alone defense, this usually is not enough to prevent the hostile bid from going through. Because the target's self-tender is usually for only a portion of the shares, tendering shareholders will be pro-rated and receive cash for only some of the shares they tender. Whereas, if they tender to the hostile bid, they generally receive cash for all of their shares. The arbitrageur has to weigh which is more valuable, the partial self-tender at a higher price, or the hostile bid for all shares, but at a lower price. This alternative presents opportunities for arbitrage.

White Knights

The preferred defense for the arbitrageur is when a target company finds a suitor of its own liking that agrees to pay a higher price, on more favorable terms than the original hostile bidder. These acquiring saviors are known as White Knights. Similar to the standstill defense, the search for a white knight usually means that the target will not remain independent. However, it is often used because it results in a transaction that is beneficial to both shareholders and management.

The arbitrageur also reaps the benefits of a higher takeover price for a target stock that he owns. The most important part of the arbitrage analysis is assessing the likelihood that a target company will actually be able to find a white knight. Has the original hostile bidder offered a high enough price that it is unlikely a competitor would bid higher? Or is there room for a white knight to pay more for the target than was originally bid? These questions faced the arbitrageurs who owned ITT Corp. stock (different from ITT Industries) as ITT tried to fend off a hostile bid from Hilton Hotels in 1997.

Hilton and ITT – The White Knight

In 1996, the share price of ITT Corp. fell from a high of $65 a share to the low $40 range, as the company was having trouble integrating its recent purchase of hotel and gaming operator Caesar's World. The weakness in the stock captured the attention of Stephen Bollenbach, CEO of Hilton Hotels.

Bollenbach attempted several times in the fall of 1996 to speak with ITT regarding a possible transaction. However, Rand Araskog, head of ITT, was not an interested seller. Having failed to negotiate a friendly deal, Bollenbach had little choice but to go hostile. On January 31, 1997, Hilton launched a $55 a share hostile tender offer for ITT. The ensuing takeover battle was a classic example of a hostile target (ITT) trying to use many of the aforementioned takeover defenses.

The day the bid was announced, arbitrageurs began paying $58 a share, $3 over Hilton's offer. The Street knew that Araskog would not go down without a fight. They also concluded that Hilton's initial bid was low relative to ITT's assets. ITT's possible defenses included selling off parts of the company and doing a self-tender for a portion of the shares, turning to a white knight in hopes of a higher bid, or negotiating a higher price. The conventional thinking was that even if a deal was not consummated, the Hilton bid would serve as a catalyst to unlock the true value of ITT, which many believed was in excess of $70 a share.

ITT's first line of defense was the poison pill it had in place. The problem was that it did not have a staggered board and its entire board of directors was up for re-election in May. To capitalize on this, Hilton launched a proxy battle to oust the ITT board. If Hilton were able to do this, it could then remove the poison pill and proceed with its offer.

Aware of its board's susceptibility, ITT moved its defense into high gear. ITT began selling off assets, including Madison Square Garden and several large hotel properties. But, Bollenbach did not go away and arbitrageurs kept buying ITT stock in anticipation of either a higher bid from Hilton or more strategic moves by ITT. They were rewarded in July when ITT announced a breakup plan into three units and a partial self-tender for $70 a share. Two weeks later, Hilton raised its bid to $70 a share.

As part of the restructuring, ITT had announced that it would stagger its board, and would do so without shareholder approval. If it were allowed to do this, Hilton would in effect be out of the game, with no way to circumvent the poison pill. But on September 29, a Nevada federal court judge ruled that ITT's restructuring required a shareholder vote. The ruling undercut ITT's defenses and opened the possibility of a Hilton slate of directors controlling the company.

With little choice left but to find a white knight, Araskog turned to Starwood Lodging. Starwood agreed to pay $82 a share ($15 cash, $67 stock) in a friendly deal for ITT. The arbitrageurs' profits continued to rise.

Hilton countered with an $80 a share bid that was 55% cash, but was outdone when Starwood raised its bid to $85. At the November shareholder meeting, the incumbent ITT board was re-elected and soon thereafter closed the deal with Starwood. Araskog's litany of defenses had thwarted the bid from Hilton but had actually enhanced returns to the arbitrageurs.

The ITT and Pennzoil deals present an interesting contrast in defense strategies and their effect on the arbitrageur's return. In the ITT case, a staunch defense actually worked extremely well for shareholders. In the Pennzoil case, the existence of unpenetrable defense mechanisms led to losses for any arbitrageur who bought Pennzoil stock after the initial bid. Because of this, it is essential that an arbitrageur understands the defenses available, how they will be used, and what effect they will have on the eventual outcome of a hostile takeover attempt. In all cases, understanding the fundamental asset values of the company in a given economic setting is important.

The **"Gabelli Magna Carta of Shareholder Rights"** (1988) lays out which of the aforementioned defenses Gabelli Funds will vote for and against:

We are in favor of:

◆ Cumulative Voting
◆ Golden Parachutes (Why? Because we want management to think about harvesting for us and not worry about its next job.)
◆ One share, one vote
◆ Cash incentives
◆ Preemptive rights

We will vote against:

◆ Greenmail
◆ Poison pills and other similar antitakeover provisions
◆ Supermajority voting
◆ Blank check preferreds
◆ Superdilutive stock options
◆ Option resets

◆ ◆ ◆

Chapter 11: Fundamental Analysis - Research

The Pharos of Alexandria (279 BC). It was the first large lighthouse ever constructed, and was so solidly built that it stood for more than 1,000 years, surviving several earthquakes.

The study of issues that can make or break a merger forms the basis of arbitrage research. Fundamental analysis plays an important role. The main reason that an arbitrageur focuses on fundamental research is to determine a fair value for the target company.

Graham and Dodd's *Security Analysis* (1934) is considered the investment bible. Benjamin Graham and David Dodd define equity research as a process of identifying companies that trade at a significant discount to their liquidation or going concern value. This discount, known as a margin of safety, provides both downside protection and significant upside when a catalyst unleashes a company's inherent value.

In merger arbitrage, that catalyst has already occurred, and fundamental analysis helps determine a fair value for the target company. If an initial bid for a company is below the target's intrinsic value, or the price at which similar transactions have gone through, the arbitrageur knows that there may be room for a higher bid. On the other hand, if a bid is richly priced relative to recent deals in the target company's industry, there may be room for the acquiring company to lower its offer, should any problems arise.

A second reason for fundamental analysis of the target is that the arbitrageur will own the target stock outright if the deal falls through. If a deal breaks, the arb must decide whether to stay long the target stock, or to sell it because there is no longer a merger agreement that insures a takeover price. That decision is facilitated by knowledge of the fundamentals of the target company.

Methods of Valuation

EBITDA

An increasingly common method of valuation is to use a multiple of earnings or EBITDA (earnings before interest, tax, depreciation, and amortization minus capital expenditures). For example, if a company had $100 million in EBITDA in its most recent fiscal year, and has received a bid of $800 million for the entire company, the buyer has offered to pay eight times EBITDA. An arbitrageur would start by comparing this multiple to the EBITDA multiple at which the target company's competitors trade. Then, even more importantly, the arb would compare the eight multiple to the multiple at which recent comparable transactions in the company's industry have been priced.

If eight times is less than the comparable companies' (comps) multiples, the target company is still somewhat cheap, and there is likely room for a higher bid. In this case, the arbitrageur is willing to invest in the deal even if the current spread is not attractive. Also in this case, if the deal breaks, there is probably less downside in the target company stock than there would be if the target were at a big premium to its peer group and other similar deals.

On the other hand, if the acquisition multiple is greater than that of the comps' multiples, the target is at a premium and the deal may be expensive. If the acquirer is paying eight times EBITDA and recent deals had been priced at at four times EBITDA, this would look like an extremely expensive transaction, concerning arbs with the downside in the target stock if the deal did not close. Such deals are not as attractive from an arbitrage standpoint. Hence, the arbs will demand a larger spread and greater potential return.

Earnings per Share

In a manner similar to that using EBITDA multiples, companies are also valued on a net earnings multiple. If a company earned $3 per share for its fiscal year and has received an offer to be bought for $90 per share, the target price is thirty times earnings. The thirty multiple should then be compared to comparable transactions in that company's industry to see if the proposed offer is in line with, above, or below recent deals.

Asset valuation measures often apply to certain industry groups such as the natural resource industry. Oil, gold, and natural gas companies may all have undervalued assets in the ground. Similarly, a company that is capital intensive may have property, plant, and equipment that has a replacement cost that is significantly higher than the value at which those are carried on the balance sheet. Finally, companies that have sizable real estate holdings may be best valued also on an asset basis.

Whatever the industry, the idea is that the true value of these assets will be realized once the company has been put in play. If the arbitrageur can calculate what the true value of the assets is, he is well on his way to determining the fairness of the acquirer's bid and the level of comfort he has being long the target stock.

Gabelli Asset Management – LIN Television and Hudson General

At Gabelli Asset Management, the arbitrage group has the benefit of an experienced fundamental research team that is familiar with many companies in the broadcasting, communications, consumer, and industrial sectors – all of which have recently been in the vortex of transactions. Because of this, when a merger deal or hostile offer is first announced, the fundamental research on the target company can be gathered and completed quickly. In many instances, the analyst covering the sector in which the deal is announced is already familiar with the company. If not familiar with the company, the analyst will at least be familiar with the industry sector and the methods of valuation that are most applicable to that sector.

Having such an advantage in fundamental research can significantly enhance the returns of a risk arbitrage fund. In underbid situations, the arbitrageur quickly becomes comfortable with the fundamentals of the target and buys its stock more aggressively, knowing that a higher bid is probable. This situation is common at Gabelli Asset Management.

The two deals discussed in this chapter, LIN Television and Hudson General, are prime examples of fundamental analysis boosting arbitrage returns. Gabelli Asset Management had large investments in both companies before they were put in play. Because the analysts at Gabelli were familiar with the fundamentals of each, the arbitrage group had the confidence to build positions after the initial bids. These positions yielded big returns in a short period of time, as higher bids came in for both companies.

LIN Television Corporation

By 1997, Gabelli Asset Management had a 20-year relationship with television broadcaster LIN Television Corporation. This included both analyst coverage of the company and an equity investment in LIN on behalf of managed accounts. The overriding issue with LIN stock in 1997 had to do with AT&T's 45% stake in the company. Before purchasing its stake in LIN, AT&T had given a "Private Market Value Guarantee" whereby AT&T agreed to either purchase the 55% of LIN TV it did not own at LIN's private market value, or put LIN up for sale by January 1998.

In a March 1997 LIN research report entitled 'I Want My PMV', Gabelli analyst Laura Linehan laid out the case for LIN TV. With the stock trading at only $41 a share in the open market, it was determined that LIN's private market value was $53 - $57 per share and that it would be realized in a reasonable period of time (because of AT&T's PMV Guarantee). The catalyst came on August 13, 1997 when buyout firm Hicks, Muse, Tate & Furst announced that it had agreed to buy LIN TV for $1.71 billion, or $47.50 a share.

On the announcement, LIN stock opened around $47 a share, leaving a small 50-cent spread for the arbitrageurs investing in the deal. While the return did not appear to be attractive at roughly 3% annualized, the analysts familiar with the company realized the significant upside in the deal. Knowing the fundamentals of LIN TV, the Gabelli arbitrage desk built a large position in the stock. Based on fundamental analysis from the research department, the arb desk saw two basic arguments for a higher bid.

The first argument involved the most common measure used for valuing broadcasting firms: placing a multiple on the company's broadcasting cash flow. The $47.50 a share Hicks bid valued LIN at 12.4x 1997 broadcasting cash flow of $140 million and only 11.4x estimated 1998 broadcasting cash flow of $150 million. These multiples were at the low end of the 12-14x range for recent television station acquisitions. If a second buyer were to pay the average multiple of only 13x, it would value LIN between $50 and

$54 a share. Having done this basic analysis, one could assume a higher bid of close to $52 a share.

At Gabelli, the analysis went one step further. Approximately 10% of LIN's broadcasting cash flow came from its LMA (Local Marketing Agreements) stations that the company did not own. These stations were startups with growth rates of close to 5 times that of the LIN's regular owned stations. Applying a fair value of close to $200 million to these stations (something that the Hicks, Muse bid did not do) brought Gabelli's expected total private market value of LIN TV up to $53-$57 a share.

In addition to this, a second argument for a higher bid was that Hicks, Muse was only a financial buyer. A strategic buyer who could realize synergistic cost savings from a LIN purchase could probably pay more than Hicks. In particular, General Electric (which owned NBC) would be a logical bidder. This was because LIN TV owned three NBC affiliates, including the company's crown jewel, KXAS in Dallas. These arguments augured strongly for a higher bid. The Gabelli analysis provided a solid underpinning to arbitrage research.

The arbitrage desk was rewarded on the position it had built at $47 a share when in early October another financial buyer, Raycom Media, bid $52.50 a share for LIN. LIN stock immediately traded up to $51 a share. Hicks, Muse responded to the Raycom bid by announcing Hicks had a powerful ally in its corner in the form of General Electric's NBC unit. NBC had agreed to purchase a majority stake in KXAS Dallas if the Hicks deal went through. Given that NBC clearly wanted to regain control of its LIN-owned affiliates and that the Raycom bid was still below Gabelli's estimated private market value, the arb desk continued buying LIN stock between $50 and $51 a share.

The buying, however, did not last long. Hicks, Muse, in conjunction with strategic buyer NBC, raised its bid to $55.71 a share just ten days later. At $55.71 a share the shareholders finally had their PMV! The deal closed in early 1998 and the Gabelli arb desk closed out an extremely profitable investment.

This deal illustrates the importance of fundamental analysis in risk arbitrage. What appeared on the surface to be a rather uninteresting spread was actually the beginning stage of a bidding war for a company that was materially undervalued. The only way to uncover this value was through insightful fundamental analysis.

In 1998, clients of Gabelli Asset Management owned 49.5% of aviation services company Hudson General. The company was an asset play, trading at a market price well below its intrinsic value. Hudson General had two primary business assets plus lots of cash.

Its main business, which the company operated through its 74% owned Hudson LLC, was aviation services. Hudson provided aircraft ground handling, refueling, and ground transportation at airports in the U.S. and Canada.

The company's other operating asset was its ownership in a Hawaiian land development venture. Through this venture, Hudson owned approximately 2000 acres of land in Hawaii.

Hudson General traded at a discount to its private market value. Seizing on the cheapness of the company's stock market price, a group of Hudson General senior managers offered to buy the company in November 1998 for $100 million. The offer was for $57.25 a share based on the 1.75 million shares outstanding. This price was just a 5% premium over the company's previous day close of $54.625 a share.

The day of the offer, arbitrageurs bid up the stock to a price of $56.375 a share. Because the spread was only 7/8 of a dollar ($57.25-$56.375), the return did not look overwhelmingly attractive. However, with the help of fundamental analysis from Gabelli's research department, the arb desk realized that buying Hudson stock at $56.375 provided an unusually attractive risk/reward opportunity. Downside was limited to the pre-deal price of $54.625, only about $1.50 lower than the current price. Potential upside was substantial.

To determine potential upside, the company could be valued on an asset basis. There were three components to the valuation of Hudson General: the company's ownership in Hudson LLC (part 1), its substantial cash balance (part 2), and its land in Hawaii (part 3).

Part 1 (Hudson LLC):

In October, the German airline Lufthansa had exercised an option it had to increase its stake in Hudson LLC from 26% to 49%. Lufthansa would pay $29.6 million for the extra 23% stake and this would reduce Hudson

General's stake in LLC from 74% to 51%. Analysts calculated that if 23% of the LLC partnership had sold for $29.6 million, the 51% that Hudson General now owned was worth $65.6 million, or $37.50 a share – without a premium for control.

In addition, the valuation had to include the proceeds Hudson would receive from having sold its 23% stake to Lufthansa. After certain adjustments, including taxes, this amount was expected to approximate $25.6 million, or $14.62 a share. The combination of the $37.50 and $14.62 valued Hudson General's investment in LLC at $52.12 a share.

Part 2 (Cash Balance):

The second and easiest part of the valuation of Hudson's assets was the company's cash balance. As of September 1998, cash and marketable securities were $36.8 million. This equated to a per share value of about $20 a share. Combining the $20 per share in cash with the $52.12 a share investment in LLC brought the total value of Hudson General to $72.12 a share. The $72 figure did not include the value of the company's land in Hawaii. It was becoming clear that there was substantial room for a higher bid and arbitrage profits.

Part 3 (Hawaiian Land):

The final piece was to value the stake Hudson had in its Hawaiian land development venture. Applying a conservative value of $2500 an acre to the 2000 acres of land the company owned in Hawaii gave a land value of $5 million. This equated to a per-share value of about $3 a share. Combining this with the previous $72.12 value yielded a final Hudson General company value of approximately $75 a share.

$75/share was well above the $57.25 that management had bid for the company. Having performed this fundamental analysis, the arbitrage group was confident of a higher bid and built a position in the stock. It prepared them well for the bidding war that ensued.

In the 14-D merger form filed by management after its November 1998 bid, Hudson wrote that it had received a letter of interest from a third party for more than the $57.25 a share offer from management. This combined with the fact the company appeared substantially undervalued again pointed to signs of a higher offer. The higher offers arrived in February 1999. First

Ranger Aerospace, a John Alden-Oppenheimer joint venture, bid $62 a share for Hudson. A week later, aviation services competitor Ogden offered $65 a share.

There were now three buyers in the race: management, Ranger, and Ogden. One obvious acquirer had not yet made a move. Lufthansa, which had just upped its stake in Hudson LLC to 49%, was unlikely to let the company go without a fight. Furthermore, Lufthansa had a history of paying up for companies. It had recently paid a large premium to purchase Sky Chefs from a Canadian investment firm. An intuitive arbitrageur would have figured this out and bought more stock in anticipation of Lufthansa joining the fray. On February 11, Lufthansa joined the game, offering $67 a share for Hudson General. It was now a four company bidding war.

In the days that followed, Ranger upped its bid to $72 a share. Finally, on February 17, Hudson General announced that it had reached an agreement to sell the company to Lufthansa for $76 a share; a value that closely approximated the fundamental analysis valuation. The arbitrageurs were receiving a 35% premium to the price at which they had bought stock ($56.375) on news of the initial bid by management back in November! This was how fundamental analysis and merger arbitrage were meant to work, hand in hand.

◆ ◆ ◆

Postscript - How to Participate in Risk ARB

Our goal in writing this book was twofold. First, we wanted to unmask what many investors view as the "black art" of arbitrage. As we have detailed, arbitrage investing involves no magic, but a disciplined, research intensive methodology in the purchase of announced mergers and acquisitions. Rigorous analysis and wise judgment comprise the science and art of successful arbitrage investing.

Since 1926, U.S. equities have returned 11.2% per year to investors. The past four years have been particularly ebullient with annual returns exceeding 20%. At some point, the equity market will return to its historical average. With that in mind, our second goal for this book was to provide insights to the benefits of investing in risk arbitrage.

We have learned that there are many advantages to investing in risk arbitrage. Risk arbitrage returns are not closely correlated with those of the stock market; they are less volatile than returns on the S&P 500; and longer term they are higher than those returns afforded by traditional investing. While these three factors provide for excellent results in the world of arbitrage, the real beauty of risk arb investing is that there is rarely a down year. Because risk arb returns consistently earn a positive return year in and year out, they fulfill the concept of a compound return. We proclaim this source of compounded earnings as the eighth wonder of the world.

You too can participate in the lucrative world of deals. The power of compounding will enhance your wealth, just as it did that of the king's sage in the rice parable.

Consistent, predictable returns through a time tested investment methodology can protect and grow your assets.

Appendix I: Risk Arbitrage Decision Tree

FIVE INITIAL QUESTIONS

1) What is the spread? What is the annualized return?
2) What are the regulatory issues/hurdles?
3) Is financing in place?
4) Is due diligence complete?
5) What is the downside if the deal breaks?

COMPANY ANALYSIS

1) Who is the buyer?
   – What is financial condition of buyer? Balance sheet, coverage ratios?
   – Reputation? History on past acquisitions?
   – Size of buyer? Will this acquisition significantly alter
     buyer strategy/structure?
   – Why does buyer want to merge…strategic, financial, etc?
   – Does acquirer own stock in the target? How much?

2) Who is the seller?
   – Financial condition of seller?
   – Nature of business of seller? Same as that of buyer?
   – What are seller's reasons for merger?
   – Are there pending litigation or environmental liabilities for the seller?

3) Combined company going forward.
   – Will transaction be accretive/dilutive? At what point will
     it become accretive?
   – Are there synergies and cost savings? How much?
   – What do the pro-forma financials look like? Does it make strategic sense?

FINANCING

1) How will merger be funded? Stock, cash, LBO?
2) Is funding in place? Is it a condition? Do they have commitments from banks?
3) Are they confident that funding will not be an issue?
4) (If a stock deal), how many shares will be issued? Very dilutive?

BACKGROUND

1) Is the deal friendly or hostile?
2) How did the merger come about? Who approached whom?
3) Did the seller put itself up for sale? If so, why?
4) Were other bidders involved? What is likelihood of a higher bid?
5) Was auction conducted? What kind? Sealed or closed bids?
6) Who were the investment banks and legal advisors for each company?

CONDITIONS

1) What are the conditions to complete the merger?
2) Is due diligence complete, or still a requirement?
3) Is there a minimum number of shares to be tendered/voted by the shareholders?
4) Under what circumstances can either company walk away from the deal?
5) Are there hurdles like revenue, profit, or sales hurdles that could impede the deal?
6) Are there debt covenants that cannot be broken by the seller?

REGULATORY ISSUES

1) Hart Scott Rodino
   – Any overlap in businesses?
   – 15 calendar days for a tender, 30 calendar days for a merger.

2) FTC/Justice Department approval
   – Will merger be anti-competitive?
   – What percent of its market's share will combined company have?

3) SEC must approve merger proxy
   – If filing must be amended, what were the issues with the initial proxy?

4) Individual state approvals
   – Insurance, healthcare, public utility

5) Specific industry approvals
   – Banks: Federal Reserve
   – Utilities: Federal Energy Regulatory Commission
   – Communications: Federal Communications Commission

6) Foreign regulatory approvals
   – European Union (EU) approval
   – Specific foreign countries' regulatory approvals

RISK vs. RETURN ISSUES

1) What is the spread on the deal? Annualized return?
2) Where will stocks go if deal breaks? What is the downside?
3) What are the odds of non-consummation of the deal? What could go wrong?
4) What are the odds that another buyer comes in and bids higher?
5) Is transaction definitive, letter of intent, or just preliminary talks?

Appendix II: Deals

Appendix II is comprised of 152 arbitrage examples. These workouts are taken directly from the Gabelli abritage funds' monthly letter, which has been writtten since 1985.

Example 1 (3/85)

Scott & Fetzer (SFZ - $60.00 - NYSE), The fund owns a position in Scott & Fetzer. Scott & Fetzer is being purchased in an LBO. The proxy has not been mailed. Here's how we calculate the rates of return.

SFZ	$62.00
Current Price	$60.00
Less Commission	$0.04
Dividends	None
Gross Profit	$1.96
Gross Profit %	3.26%
Holding Period (expect a May 15 payment)	53 days
Simple return	3.26%
Annualized Rate of Return	22.45%

Example 2 (4/85)

Gulf Broadcast (GBCO - $14 7/8 - OTC) - is in the process of liquidation. The major assets consist of broadcasting properties and real estate. GBCO has agreed to sell the broadcasting units to Taft Broadcasting for $760 million, and the real estate holdings to Gibraltar Savings Association for $126 million. After these transactions close, GBCO plans to liquidate, resulting in a series of distributions to shareholders.

Net Assets:	Value (millions)
Broadcast Properties, Land & Other Assets	$979.4
Cash Flow Retained by Seller	30.0
Less: Long Term Debt	(213.0)
Other Liabilities	(75.7)
Net Assets	$720.70
Per Share	
(44.5 million shares)	$16.18

Expected Rate of Return:

GBCO	$16.18
Current Price	14.87
Plus Commission	0.04
Gross Profit	$1.27
Gross Profit %	8.52%
Holding Period (Days)	
10/15/85 176	$15.00
1/2/86 254	.93
5/31/87 768	.25
Annualized Rate of Return	19.00%

Example 3 (5/85)

MGM/UA Home Entertainment (HEG - $27 3/8 - NYSE) The fund owns a position in MGM/UA Home Entertainment. MGM/UA Entertainment is acquiring the 15% of HEG it does not already own. The proxy will be mailed to shareholders in time for the June 14 shareholders' meeting. The closing of the business combinations will follow promptly thereafter. Here's how we calculate the rates of return:

HEG	$28.00
Current Price	27 3/8
Less Commission	$0.04
Dividends	None
Gross Profit	.585
Gross Profit %	2.13%
Holding Period (expect a June 28 payment)	36 Days
Annualized Rate of Return	21.69%

Example 4 (7/85)

Storer Communications (SCI - $80 5/8 - NYSE) The fund has a position in Storer Communications. The management of Storer, along with Kohlberg Kravis Roberts & Co., is doing a leveraged buyout of Storer. The Group is offering to pay $75 in cash plus a $25 face value preferred share, which will pay a 13% dividend starting at the end of the sixth year, plus a warrant to purchase 1/10th of one common share of the new company over a ten year period after a public offering has taken place for each Storer share.

Timing is dictated by financing arrangements, SEC clearance and most importantly, FCC clearance. We expect a mid-December close.

With these assumptions of values and timing, here's how we calculate the rates of return:

Cash	$75.00
Preferred	$10.00
Warrant	$2.50
	$87.50
Current Price	$80.625
Less Commission	0.04
Dividends (2)	0.20
Net Value	$80.865
Gross Profit	7.035
Gross Profit %	8.70%
Holding Period (expect a December 15 payment)	146 days
Annualized Rate of Return	21.8%

104

Example 5 (8/85)

United Energy Resources (UER - $40 1/4 - NYSE)   Midcon is acquiring United Energy through a two-step buyout. The first step is a $41 cash tender offer for 65% of the outstanding shares. The remaining 35% of the shares are to be acquired through a merger, whereby $41 worth of Midcon stock will be exchanged for each share of United Energy. A $0.62 dividend will be paid on 100% of our shares. The key to estimating our expected rate of return is to determine where the "backend" stock, (i.e. our remaining shares after the cash tender offer) will trade following the tender period of the deal. The ultimate value of the merger step (2nd step) must be discounted back at an acceptable rate of return to the time of the tender period in order to figure out where the backend stock trades.

UER	
Value of Tender = $41 x .65 =	$26.65
Value of "Backend" = 39.50 x .35 =	13.83
($41 Discounted back to the Tender Period from 11/15 at 20%	
Total	$40.48
Plus Dividend	0.62
Less Commission	(0.04)
Net Value	$41.06
Current Price	$40.25
Gross Profit	.81
Gross Profit %	2.00%
Holding Period (expect a September 20 payment)	15 days
Annualized Rate of Return	48.3%

Example 6 (12/85)

Beatrice Companies (BRY - $46 1/4 - NYSE)   Kohlberg Kravis Roberts & Co. is acquiring Beatrice through a leveraged buyout. Shareholders will receive $43 per share in cash, $7 per share in value of a preferred stock. In addition, a $.45 per share dividend has been declared. The preferred stock is to have a $7 value on a "fully-distributed" basis. For the sake of conservatism we will assume the security has a market value of $6.50 at the consummation date. The transaction is subject to financing and shareholder approval. We expect to get paid by mid-March 1986.

BRY Cash	$43.00
Preferred	$6.50
Total	$49.50
Plus Dividend	.45
Less commission	(.04)
Net Value	$49.91
Current Price	$46.25
Gross Profit	3.66
Gross Profit %	7.91%
Holding Period (expect a 3/15/86 payment)	92 days
Annualized Rate of Return	31.4%

Example 7 (1/86)

MTV Networks (MTVN - $32 3/4 - OTC) Viacom International acquired a two-thirds interest in MTV from Warner Amex (Warner Communications) in November of 1985. Also in November, Viacom agreed to acquire the remaining one-third interest from public shareholders in a $33.50 cash merger. To complete the transaction MTV and Viacom must file an information statement (versus a proxy statement since Viacom already has sufficient control to approve the merger) with the SEC. Once the document is filed a 10-day waiting period begins during which the SEC can review the proposal. MTV can subsequently mail the information statement to shareholders. After twenty days (number of days depends on the state of incorporation) following the mailing, the merger can close. The FCC and the FTC have already approved the combination. We expect the filing to take place mid to late January and we expect a closing of mid to late February.

MTVN - Sale Price	$33.50
Plus Dividend	.00
Net Value	$33.50
Current Price	$32.75
Plus Commission	.04
Acquisition Cost	$32.79
Gross Profit	.71
Gross Profit %	2.17%
Holding Period (expect a 2/28/86 payment)	42 days
Annualized Rate of Return	18.86%

Example 8 (2/86)

RCA (RCA - $61 3/4 - NYSE) In December RCA agreed to be acquired by General Electric in a $66.50 cash merger. GE has three major hurdles it must pass before it completes the transaction. The first is to receive RCA shareholder approval, which is scheduled for February 13th. The second is FTC/Justice Department clearance. GE received a second HSR request in late January and therefore the deal will probably not receive the go-ahead until at least the end of February. The final and most time consuming obstacle is FCC approval, which could take eight to ten months. To be conservative we expect a mid-October closing. We anticipate receiving three $0.26 dividends during the holding period. Our expected profit will be taxed as a long term gain.

RCA - Sale Price	$66.50
Plus Dividends	.78
Net Value	$67.28
Current Price	$61.75
Plus Commissions	.04
	$61.79
Gross Profit	$5.49
Gross Profit %	8.89%
Holding Period (expect a 10/15/86 payment)	239 days
Annualized Rate of Return	13.58%

Example 9 (3/86)

Sheller-Globe (SHG - $45.00 - NYSE) General Felt has agreed to acquire Sheller-Globe through a leveraged buyout transaction. Shareholders are to receive $39 in cash and $17 face value in a zero coupon for five years, 15 1/2% thereafter subordinated debenture. Presently, we think the debenture will trade at about $7.50 per share. In addition, we anticipate receiving a $0.225 dividend. The deal is subject to financing, which General Felt already has firm commitments for, and shareholder approval. The latter requires a proxy to be filed, cleared by the SEC and mailed to shareholders. We expect a mid-to-late May closing.

SHG - Sale Price	
Cash	$39.00
Debenture	7.50
	$46.50
Plus Dividend	.225
Net Value	$46.725
Current Price	$45.00
Plus Commissions	.04
	45.04
Gross Profit	$1.685
Gross Profit %	3.74%
Holding Period (expect a 5/23/86 payment)	67 days
Annualized Rate of Return	20.38%

Example 10 (4/86)

National Gypsum (NG - $49 1/2 - NYSE) National Gypsum has agreed to be acquired by its management through a leveraged buyout. We are to receive $41 in cash and $17 face amount in a five year zero, 15.5% thereafter subordinated debenture. The debentures have been trading "when issued" at a 53 cents on the dollar level, or about $9.00 (net of commissions) per share of National Gypsum. We, therefore, sell the W.I. paper at 53 and lock in a total value of $50.00. No dividend will be paid and we are assuming that full payment will be made within two weeks after the shareholder vote, which is scheduled for April 10th.

NG - Sale Price	
Cash	$41.00
Debenture	9.00
	$50.00
Plus Dividend	0.00
Net Value	$50.00
Current Price	49.50
Plus Commissions	.04
	$49.54
Gross Profit	0.46
Gross Profit %	0.93%
Holding Period (expect a 4/24/86 payment)	14 days
Annualized Rate of Return	24.21%

Example 11 (5/86)

Union Carbide Consumer Division Rights (UK - RT - $32 1/2 - NYSE) Union Carbide announced in January that it was going to sell its consumer products division and subsequently distribute, to shareholders, the excess of the net selling price less the division's book value. Carbide entered into a definitive agreement with Ralston Purina to sell its battery business, and with First Boston to sell its Home and Auto businesses. A $33.20 per share distribution will be paid following the completion of the two transactions. The sales are scheduled to close by June 30, and the distribution will be made a week or two later. Additionally, if Carbide receives a favorable court opinion disallowing certain of its employee compensation plans from the distribution, shareholders will receive another $0.85 per share. Also, the Indian subsidiary of the battery division has yet to be sold due to the Bhopal legal battle. With a book value of $20 million ($0.63 per share), the net selling price of the business will be distributed to shareholders when and if it is sold. Both of these contingent payments are most likely at least a year off. The idea in buying the rights is to earn a return that will at least cover the cost of carry based on the $33.20 distribution, and then possibly realize one or two small, but delightful, "kisses" at some point further into the future.

UK-RT Expected Net Proceeds	$33.20
Current Price	$32.50
Plus Commissions	0.04
	$32.54
Gross Profit	0.66
Gross Profit %	2.03%
Holding Period (expect a 7/15/86 payment)	64 days
Annualized Rate of Return	11.57%

Example 12 (6/86)

Sperry Corp (SY - $74 5/8 - NYSE) is in a definitive agreement to be acquired by Burroughs in a $76.50 two-stepped buyout. The first step is a $76.50 cash tender offer for 50% of the fully diluted outstanding shares. On the "backend", or merger portion of the transaction, the remaining 50% of the shares will be exchanged into $38.25 face amount of 9 3/4 subordinated debentures plus .765 of a share of Burroughs 7½% convertible preferred with a total implied value of $76.50 per share on a "fully-distributed" basis. For the sake of conservatism we will assume that the securities have a total market value of $76.00 at the consummation date. A $0.48 dividend will be paid on the "backend" shares. The key to estimating our expected rate of return is to determine where the "backend" stock will trade following the tender portion of the deal. The ultimate value of the merger step must be discounted back at an acceptable rate of return to the time of the tender period in order to figure out where the "backend" stock trades.

SY	
Value of Tender = 76.50 x .50	$38.25
Value of "Backend" = 74.26 x .50	37.13
($76.00) + $0.48 dividend discounted back to the tender period	
from August 15 at 20%)	
Total	75.38
Current Price	$74.63
Plus Commission	.04
	74.67
Gross Profit	0.71
Gross Profit %	0.01%
Holding Period (expect a 6/23/86 payment)	14 days
Annualized Rate of Return	24.79%

Example 13 (7/86)

Fruehauf (FTR - $47 7/8 - NYSE) has agreed to be acquired by a Merrill Lynch group in a $48.50 two-stepped leveraged buyout. The first step is a $48.50 cash tender offer for 78% of the fully diluted outstanding shares. On the "backend", or merger portion of the transaction, the remaining 22% of the shares will be exchanged into $43.50 face amount of a $3.56 exchangeable redeemable preferred stock and one share of a Class B Common Stock of the new company. The terms of the preferred are almost identical to the preferred issued from the Beatrice LBO, except that a stock dividend will be paid for five years rather than six, and the stock will have a dividend yield on face value of 14.25% rather than 15.25%. The Beatrice paper is trading slightly above face value and we anticipate that the Fruehauf paper may follow suit once it is fully distributed. We expect the Class B Common to trade at least at its implied value of $5.00. The market may attach a premium to a security that enables the public holder to participate in an LBO, as in the case of Multimedia. At this time, we anticipate the "backend" will have a market value equivalent to its implied value of $48.50 at the consummation date.

FTR

Value of Tender = 48.50 x .78	$37.83
Value of "Backend" = 46.81 x .22	10.30
($48.50 + $0.175 dividend	
discounted back to the tender period from September 30 at 20%)	
Total	48.13
Current Price	$47.88
Plus Commission	0.04
	47.92
Gross Profit	0.21
Gross Profit %	0.004%
Holding Period (expect a 8/1/86 payment)	10 days
Annualized Rate of Return	16.00%

Example 14 (8/86)

Safeway (SA - $65 1/2 - NYSE) has agreed to be acquired by Kohlberg, Kravitz and Roberts (KKR) in a two-stepped leveraged buyout. In the first step we are to receive $69 in a cash tender offer for 73.5% of the outstanding shares. In the second step we are to receive $61.60 value on a fully distributed basis in a five year zero coupon debenture and a 10-year warrant that will enable us to buy an equity interest in the new company. The total warrant issue will enable the public shareholders to buy a 5% interest at twice the KKR cost. We are estimating the present value of the warrant at between $1.00 and $1.50 per share. At the merger date we anticipate the debentures may have a trading value of $61.00 and the warrants a trading value of $1.00.

SA

Value of Tender = 69.00 x .735 =	$50.72
Value of "Backend" = 59.00 x .265 =	15.64
($61.00 + $1.00 + $0.425 dividend discounted	
back to the tender period from November 28 at 20%)	
Total	66.35
Current Price	$65.50
Plus Commission	0.04
	65.54
Gross Profit	0.85
Gross Profit %	1.3%
Holding Period (expect a 9/8/86 payment)	19 days
Annualized Rate of Return	24.04%

Example 15 (9/86)

Big Three Industries (BIG - $28 3/8 - NYSE) has agreed to be acquired by L'Air Liquide in a $29 cash tender offer. The major obstacle to the deal is getting FTC approval. L'Air received a second HSR request on September 2. Once L'Air is deemed by the FTC to have complied with the second request, a 10 calendar day waiting period begins. At the end of the waiting period, if the FTC hasn't filed suit to halt the transaction, the tender offer can be completed. We anticipate L'Air will comply with the second request by the end of September. We would therefore expect to get paid by the middle of October. A $0.22 dividend may be declared in early October.

	Without Dividend	With Dividend
BIG	$29.00	$29.00
Plus Dividend	0.00	0.22
Net Value	29.00	29.22
Current Price	$28.375	0.04
Plus Commission	28.415	28.415
Gross Profit	0.585	0.805
Gross Profit %	2.06%	2.83%
Holding Period (expect a 10/15/86 payment)	30 days	30 days
Annualized Rate of Return	25.05%	34.47%

Example 16 (10/86)

Hammermill Paper (HML - $64.00 - NYSE), in September, International Paper acquired roughly 94% of Hammermill Paper in a $64.50 tender offer. The remaining 6% of the shares, which did not tender into the offer for one reason or another, will be acquired by International in a statutory merger. Since they own more than 90% of the shares, IP can do a "short-form" merger, which requires SEC clearance, but takes less time and effort to accomplish than a "standard" merger. This is what we call a "backend deal". Our risk is relatively low; primarily a time risk. Since only a small percentage of the shares remain outstanding after the tender offer and many of those shares are dormant (which is why they weren't tendered in the first place), the stock trades very thin, and so it's difficult to buy a large quantity of stock. Nevertheless, we bid for the stock at a chosen price level and occasionally buy a sizeable piece. We expect a mid-November merger date and subsequent close.

HML	$64.50
Plus Dividend	0.00
Net Value	64.50
Current Price	$64.00
Plus Commission	0.04
	64.04
Gross Profit	0.46
Gross Profit %	0.718%
Holding Period (expect a 11/14/86 payment)	16 days
Annualized Rate of Return	16.39%

Example 17 (12/86)

Viacom International (VIA - $38 1/2 - NYSE) in October, Viacom agreed to be acquired in a management-led leveraged buyout. We are to receive $37 in cash, $7 value (on a fully distributed basis) in a preferred stock and a unit that represents an equity stake in the new company (the issue in aggregate will represent 20% of the equity). At the merger date we anticipate the preferred stock will have a trading value of about $6.50. We are estimating the value of the equity unit to be about $1.00. The proxy was filed with the SEC in late November for a shareholder vote that should take place in early February. This transaction also requires FCC approval. The buyout group filed a license transfer request with the FCC in early November. The FCC subsequently received one complaint against the transfer. Due to the complaint, the FCC approval could take another two to three months. The Group has sufficient commitments from lenders to complete the deal. However, a portion of the financing is to come from "high yield" (junk) securities. In the current environment we are not sure how much relevance the word "commitment" has. In addition, we are concerned about "pencil sharpening" relative to the new tax bill. All in all, we expect the transaction to close in late March. Nonetheless, the larger than "normal spread" is primarily the result of the complexity of this deal relative to the various hurdles that must be crossed. Concerns over business prospects also adds to the spread.

VIA	
Cash	$37.00
Preferred Stock	6.50
Equity Unit	1.00
	$44.50
Plus Dividend	0.07
Net Value	44.57
Current Price	$38.50
Plus Commission	0.04
	38.54
Gross Profit	6.03
Gross Profit %	15.65%
Holding Period (expect a 3/31/87 payment)	89 days
Annualized Rate of Return	64.17%

Example 18 "The Back End" (1/87)

Ryan Homes (RYN - $46 1/4 - NYSE) In November, Ryan Homes agreed to be acquired in a $48 two-stepped buyout by NV Homes. The first step was a $48 cash tender for about 53% of the outstanding shares. The tender expired December 2. In the second step, or merger step, we are to receive $41.75 in cash and $6.25 value in NV Home units (NV Homes is a limited partnership, not a corporation and so we will receive L.P. units and not common stock). The number of NV Home units that we ultimately will receive will depend upon a 10 day price averaging period prior to the merger. Since NV is a thinly traded stock we expect to have a difficult time shorting any of the stock during the pricing period. We therefore assume we will lose about $0.50 of the $6.50 value while "unwinding" from our position. The proxy is expected to be filed by the end of this month for a late March shareholder vote. But delays with the SEC are common, and so we don't expect a closing until mid-April. However, if the closing date does go into April, we will probably receive another $0.30 dividend. The major risk in the deal at this point is getting out of NV Homes without losing too much of the $6.50 value".

RYN	
Cash	$41.75
NV Homes ("$6.25 Value")	5.75
	$47.50
Plus Dividend	0.30
Net Value	47.80
Current Price	$46.25
Plus Commission	0.04
	46.29
Gross Profit	1.51
Gross Profit %	3.26%
Holding Period (expect a 4/15/87 payment)	79 days
Annualized Rate of Return	15.07%

Example 19 (2/87)

Hazelton Laboratories (HLC - $29 1/4 - NYSE) - A "Collar" Hazelton Laboratories agreed to be acquired by Corning Glass Works in a $30 stock merger. We are to receive $30 worth of Glass Works common stock with a minimum of .4918 shares but no more than .5882 shares. This .4918-.5882 is known as the "collar" of the deal. If Glass Works is below $51 at the merger date then our considerations will be worth less than $30. On the other hand, if Glass Works is above $61 at the merger date, our consideration will be more than $30. The proxy was filed February 10 for a tentative March 31 shareholder vote. With slippage and the settlement of selling the new stock after it is received, we expect payment in Mid-April.

HLC	$30.00
Plus Dividend	0.10
Net Value	$30.10
Current Price	$29.25
Plus Commission	0.04
	29.29
Gross Profit	0.81
Gross Profit %	2.77%
Holding Period (expect a 4/15/87 payment)	51 days
Annualized Rate of Return	19.79%

112

Example 20 (3/87)

Piedmont Aviation (PIE - $67 5/8 - NYSE) agreed to be acquired by USAir for $69 in cash. If USAir is granted a 100% voting trust by the Department of Transportation (DOT), 100% of the outstanding shares will be accepted in a $69 cash tender. If the DOT follows its past practices of granting only a 51% voting trust, USAir will tender for approximately 46.5% of the shares they don't already own. For the remaining shares, USAir will pay $69 in cash plus interest on the amount at an annual rate of 5.5% until the merger is concluded. Shareholder approval and formal DOT approval are required before the close. The latter requisite could take as long as six months. The object from our point of view is to pay a price that would earn us an exceptional rate of return if the 100% trust is granted, and a low, but acceptable rate of return if only the 51% trust is granted.

	100% Trust	51% Trust Front	51% Trust Back
PIE	$69.00	$69.00	$69.00
Plus Interest	0.00	0.00	1.56
Net Value	69.00	69.00	70.56
Current Price	$67.625		
Plus commission	0.04		
	67.665	67.665	67.665
Gross Profit	1.335	1.335	2.895
Gross Profit %	1.97%	1.97%	4.28%
Holding Period (expect a 4/9/87 payment and a 9/15/87 payment)	14 Days	14 Days	168 Days
Annualized Rate of Return	51.44%	51.44%	9.30%
Internal Rate of Return	51.44%		13.5%

Example 21 (4/87)

Heritage Communications (HCI - $33.00 - NYSE) agreed to be acquired by Telecommunications Inc. and Heritage management in a $32 merger. We are to receive $26 in cash and $8 in TCI stock. Alternatively, TCI has the option to give us all cash. The transaction requires shareholder approval, FCC approval and a variety of cable system consents. Shareholder approval is expected in late May, while the FCC approval and the cable consents are expected by early June. We anticipate a mid-June close. Although we are using $8.00, the stock portion of the consideration is not a "hard" value, and therefore, our expected value is subject to a minor adjustment.

HCI Cash	$26.00
Stock	8.00
Plus Dividend	0.01
Net Value	34.01
Current Price	$33.00
Plus Commission	0.04
	33.04
Gross Profit	0.97
Gross Profit %	2.94%
Holding Period (expect a 6/15/87 payment)	47 Days
Annualized Rate of Return	22.83%

Example 22 (5/87)

GenCorp (GY - $115 1/4 - NYSE) has offered to purchase about 55% of its outstanding shares for $130. The other 45% of the shares will remain outstanding as the company continues to trade publicly. In order to eliminate our market risk, we are buying put options (in this case, June 100 puts) to protect 45% of our position (our backend). Subsequent to the tender expiration if the new stock trades below 100, then we will lose $0.61 per share. If the stock trades better than 100, our spread improves. As stated earlier, if the prorate improves, our spread will improve accordingly.

		Backend	
GY	< 100	105	110
Front End ($130 X 55%)	$71.50	$71.50	$71.50
Back End (Value X 45%)	45.00	47.25	49.50
Net Value	116.50	118.75	121.00
Current Price	$115.25	$115.25	$115.25
Plus Cost of Put ($4 X 45%)	1.80	1.80	1.80
Plus Commission	0.06	0.06	0.06
	117.11	117.11	117.11
Gross Profit	(0.61)	1.64	3.89
Gross Profit %	(0.52%)	1.4%	3.32%
Holding Period	-----	18 days ----	
(expect a 5/26/87 payment)			
Annualized Rate of Return	(10.56%)	28.39%	67.36%

Example 23 (6/87)

Harcourt Brace Jovanovich (HBJ - $58.00 - NYSE) has announced a recapitalization that includes paying shareholders a special $40 cash dividend plus $13.50 face amount of a 12% preferred while retaining the original share in the company. The issuance of the preferred requires shareholder approval which is expected to take place in mid-July. We feel that the preferred will have a market value of $10.00. The cash and the preferred will be paid to shareholders on July 27. The "new" company has begun trading on a "when-issued" basis. We can buy the regular way stock and sell the when-issued stub in order to lock in a spread.

HBJ	
Cash	$40.00
Preferred	10.00
W.I. Stub	10.25
Net Value	$60.25
Current Price	$58.00
Plus Commission	0.04
	58.04
Gross Profit	2.21
Gross Profit %	3.81%
Holding Period (expect a 7/31/87 payment)	44 days
Annualized Rate of Return	31.59%

114

Example 24 (7/87)

Taft Broadcasting (TFB - $152.00 - NYSE) has agreed to be acquired by a group that includes Carl Lindner (through FMI Financial), the Bass family and Dudley Taft (as well as other Taft family members) in a $157 cash merger. Shareholders have the option to take $144 in cash and one share of FMI Financial, which trades on NASDAQ (FMIF-13 3/4). The transaction requires FCC and shareholder approvals. The FCC license transfer application has been filed and the comment period expires July 15. We expect a September 30 close.

TFB	$157.00
Plus: Dividend	0.29
Net Value	157.29
Current Price	$152.00
Plus commission	0.04
	152.04
Gross Profit	5.25
Gross Profit %	3.45%
Holding Period (expect a 9/30/87 payment)	75 days
Annualized Rate of Return	16.80%

Example 25 (8/87)

Adams Russell (AAR - $40 1/2 - NYSE) has agreed to be acquired by Cablevision Systems in a $43.075 cash merger. The transaction is subject to shareholder, FCC and cable system locality approvals. We expect a mid to late October shareholder vote and an early December close. The major hurdle is getting local government consents on the ownership change of 130 odd cable systems.

AAR	$43.075
Plus: Dividend	0.000
Net Value	43.075
Current Price	$40.50
Plus Commission	0.04
	40.540
Gross Profit	2.535
Gross Profit %	6.253%
Holding Period (expect a December 11 close)	115 days
Annualized Rate of Return	19.85%

Example 26 (9/87)

Southland Corp. (SLC - $75.00) has agreed to be acquired by Thompson Co. in a two-stepped buyout (as detailed in update #9). The tender offer, or first step, has passed. For the second step, we are to receive $61.32 in cash and $16.68 face amount in a 15% 5 year PIK (payment-in-kind) preferred. The preferred has call protection for two years (in the form of a $0.75 premium), which is unusual for merger paper. Furthermore, if the new Southland goes public within two years, the company will offer each initial recipient of the preferred shares the one-time opportunity to subscribe on a prorata basis to an aggregate of up to 25% of the offering at a discount of 10% from the public offering price. But most important in terms of the quality of the preferred is the financial strength of the new company going forward. Based on the company's projections, Southland should have more than ample cash flow to meet its future obligations. For the sake of conservatism we will assume that the preferred initially trades at $0.95 on the dollar, or $16.00 per Southland share. The proxy was filed on August 27. We anticipate a mid-November close.

SLC Cash	$61.32
Preferred ($16.68 X 95)	16.00
Plus: Dividend	0.00
Net Value	77.32
Current Price	$75.00
Plus Commission	0.04
	75.04
Gross Profit	2.28
Gross Profit %	3.04%
Holding Period (expect a November 16 close)	56 days
Annualized Rate of Return	19.80%

Example 27 (11/87)

Argonaut Group (AGII- $29.00) In early October, Argonaut Group agreed to be acquired in an LBO led by Gibbons, Green, van Amerongen. Shareholders are to receive $45 in cash and $8 value in a preferred stock. The merger is subject to shareholder approval and regulatory approval. Argonaut is in the property and casualty insurance business and thus the buyout will require insurance commission approvals in each of the states in which the company does business, (California, Georgia, Idaho, Illinois and Louisiana). The merger is also subject to obtaining financing. In the current environment this condition is by far the most onerous. The huge spread in the stock reflects that fact. However, the downside from this level may not be that substantial. At $29, Argonaut is in a trading range that is comparable to the current trading levels of other insurance concerns based on a standard multiple analysis. The proxy has not been filed and appears to be on hold until a workable financing plan can be put in place. The current intention is to close before the end of the first quarter of 1988. We will use March 31 as our target.

AGII Cash	$45.00
Preferred ($8.00 x .50)	4.00
Plus: Dividend	0.00
Net Value	49.00
Current Price	$29.00
Plus commission	0.04
	29.04
Gross Profit	19.96
Gross Profit %	68.73%
Holding Period (expect a March 31 close)	128 days
Annualized Rate of Return	195.99%

Example 28   (12/87)

CNW Corp. (CNW- $22 1/2) agreed to be acquired in a management buyout led by Gibbons Green (the same group attempting an LBO of Argonaut - Example 27). Shareholders are to receive $20 in cash, $9 value in a 5 year PIK note and $2 value in the equity of the new company. Although the note is to be priced at the close to give us a $9 value we will haircut the intention by $2 to take into account the current environment for high yield securities. The equity piece is a fair $2 since it's the same price Gibbons Green and management are paying for their interest. The merger requires ICC and shareholder approvals. The proxy should be filed later this month for a mid-March close. The large spread reflects the risk premium currently being attached to leveraged deals by the market in addition to concerns over the labor issues effecting CNW.

CNW	
Cash	$20.00
Note	7.00
Equity	2.00
Plus: Dividend	0.00
Net Value	29.00
Current Price	$22.50
Plus Commission	0.04
	22.54
Gross Profit	6.46
Gross Profit %	28.66%
Holding Period (expect a March 15 close)	83 days
Annualized Rate of Return	126.04%

Example 29 (3/88)

Mobile Communications Corp. of America (MCCAB - $26 3/8) agreed to be acquired by Bell South in a $28.75 stock merger. In addition to the $28.75 in Bell South stock, shareholders will receive a share in a new company that represents the non-cellular and non-paging assets of Mobile. The new company will have a book value of $2.00 per share. For the sake of conservatism, we will assume a $2.00 trading value for the spinoff. Bell South must cross a number of hurdles in order to complete the deal. A merger proxy and an information statement (for the spinoff) are required to be filed with the SEC and mailed to shareholders.

More importantly, Bell South needs to obtain numerous government regulatory approvals since both the cellular telephone and the paging industries are highly regulated. The FCC must sign off to the transactions as well as sixteen of the states in which Mobile operates in. Finally, and likely the most lengthy approval required, is the blessing of Judge Harold Green, the man who was assigned the task of overseeing, among other things, this type of extraordinary transaction by any of the "Baby Bells". Though all of these approvals will take time, we feel confident that they will be granted. Over the last two years, two other successful transactions (PacTel acquisition of Communications Industries and Southwestern Bell's acquisition of Metromedia Cellular) involved a "Baby Bell" purchase of a cellular concern. Based on history, our best estimate is a late October close.

MCCAB Stock	$28.75
Spinoff	2.00
Plus: Dividend	0.00
Net Value	30.75
Current Price	$26.375
Plus Commission	0.04
	26.42
Gross Profit	4.33
Gross Profit %	16.41%
Holding Period (expect an October 31 close)	230 days
Annualized Rate of Return	26.04%

Example 30 (4/88)

Federated Department Stores (FDS $71 3/4) is in a definitive agreement to be acquired by Campeau Corp. in a $73.50 tender. As previously noted, up until the end of March, Federated was involved in a complex, hotly contested bidding war between Campeau and Macys (which, by the way, could be material for a terrific epic T.V. mini-series). Now we are left with a simple, 'If friendly" tender offer. Financing commitments have been secured and the FTC has given the transaction its blessing. The tender is scheduled to expire on April 20 (but more than likely will be extended until May 12). The primary reason that we chose the now "boring" Federated deal as an example is to illustrate the profitability of the risk arbitrage environment over the last few months. The expected annualized rate of return of 37.8% for this friendly fully financed deal compares most favorably to the 18-19% expected rates of return that we could hope for a year ago. The Federated size spreads are primarily a function of having many deals on the board currently (hot money moves fast) coupled with fewer dollars to close the spreads (a result of the October casualties). Though the reinvestment of profits earned over the last three months has increased the arbitrage community's pool of funds, we see no evidence of a slow down in deal activity and therefore no reason to think spreads will materially shrink.

FDS	$73.50
Plus: Dividend	0.00
Net Value	73.50
Current Price	$71.75
Plus Commission	0.04
	71.79
Gross Profit	1.71
Gross Profit %	2.38%
Holding Period (expect a May 12 payment close)	23 days
Annualized Rate of Return	37.80%

Example 31 (6/88)

USG Corp. (USG - 47 1/8 - NYSE) has announced a recapitalization plan that calls for shareholders to receive $37 in cash, $5 face amount of a 16% 5 year PIK debenture and one share in the ongoing company. Shareholders are to approve the plan at a July 8 meeting. Since the proxy is effective, the two securities that will emanate from the plan are trading on a "when-issued" basis. Rather than try to estimate what the two securities are worth we can simply sell them on a "when-issued" basis in order to lock-in an attractive spread.

USG Cash	$ 37.000
Debenture (at 103)	5.150
Stub (at 6 1/8)	6.125
Net Value	48.275
Current Price	$47.125
Plus commission	0.04
	47.165
Gross Profit	1.11
Gross Profit %	2.35%
Holding Period (expect a July 20 payment)	24 days
Annualized Rate of Return	35.79%

Example 32 (7/88)

GAF Corp. (GAF - $45.00) is in the midst of a management led LBO valued at $51 per share. Shareholders are to receive $46 in cash and $5 value in a subordinated debenture (which we estimate will have an initial trading value of about $4.50). Management initially proposed an LBO back in September of 1987 worth about $66.50 per share. The October crash caused (or perhaps allowed) management to withdraw the proposal but hinted that the LBO could be resurrected at some point in the future. Sure enough, in February of this year management suited back up in their LBO attire and proposed a buyout, but at a much lower price of $51 per share in cash and paper. Whether or not a lower price is justified is unclear. Business for GAF appears to be unaffected by the "crash" (just reported another record quarter) and financing (both bank and junk) is cheaper than it was back in September of last year. Furthermore, between October and the early part of this year management was shrewd enough to cause the corporation to buy back in the open market over 17% of the outstanding shares at an average price of roughly $37.50 per share; effectively reducing the ultimate cost of the company to management of close to $80 million.

Subsequent to the announcement of the lower offer, the stock traded at a tight spread and even at a premium to the bid because of the "street" consensus that the deal was readily do-able, and could even attract competing bidders.

The "street's" confidence however, quickly evaporated when both GAF and one of its top executives were indicted by the Feds of alleged stock manipulation in the selling of a large block of Union Carbide. Criminal indictments are a legitimate cause of concern as to whether or not the LBO will ever be completed. Prospective bank lenders for the deal to take an may show more than a little pause example, in deciding whether to participate in the buyout when the future liability of these criminal (and potential civil) proceedings are unquantifiable let alone the possibility that one or more of GAF's top executives may be making license plates rather than business decisions for the next couple of years. These concerns are the reason GAF is trading at $45, a $6 spread for a deal that could close in about 70 days. On the other side of the coin, at $45, the stock appears to be trading in a range that could be supported by its fundamentals relative to other comparable chemical concerns. If the deal were to be terminated tomorrow, the downside would probably not be too painful. If the flip side occurs, we will have earned a tremendous return.

Example 33 (8/88)

AMFAC INC. (AMA - $46 1/4 - NYSE) has agreed to be acquired by JMB Realty in a cash merger. Shareholders are to receive $49 per share. The merger is conditioned upon shareholder approval. The proxy will be filed by the end of August and may take approximately five weeks to pass through the SEC. The proxy should then in turn get mailed in early October for an early November vote and subsequent close. If the merger does not close by November 7, JMB will accrue interest on the $49 at a rate of 7%, therefore we are somewhat protected if a delay occurs.

We are somewhat troubled that the takeover is being effected through a merger rather than a tender offer. Though JMB has commitments for the financing, three months can approach eternity when it comes to financial market stability. Furthermore, the Hawaiian government can be uncooperative when it comes to real estate holders, which AMFAC is in a major way. These potential problem areas are the reason for the relatively rich spread. On the other hand, during the auction of the company, numerous parties expressed an interest in bidding for the company and so the potential still remains for a higher bid. For the time being we will hold only a modest position until further developments.

AMA	
Cash	$49.00
Dividend	0.00
Net Value	49.00
Current Price	$46.25
Plus commission	.0.04
	46.29
Gross Profit	2.71
Gross Profit %	5.85%
Holding Period (expect a November 8 payment)	78 days
Annualized rate of return	27.38%

Example 34 (9/88)

Farmers Group (FGRP - $71 1/4 - NYSE) has agreed to be acquired by B.A.T. in a $75 cash merger (see update #7 for the background). In addition to getting a proxy to shareholders, B.A.T. must get approval from the insurance commissions of the nine states in which Farmers operates. Other than getting a reaffirmation of approval from a few states (to approve the higher price and structure), B.A.T. is waiting for Texas, Kansas and Oregon to approve the merger. It appears that Oregon may present a hurdle, as the commissioner in that state previously rejected the takeover (before it became friendly) on very broad grounds. In any case, Oregon represents only a approximately 3% of Farmers Group's business, so the state will not be a show stopper. We see a close by year end.

FGRP	Cash	$75.00
	Dividend	0.36
Net Value		75.36
Current Price	$71.25	
Plus Commission	0.04	
		71.29
Gross Profit		4.07
Gross Profit %		5.71%
Holding Period (expect a December 31 payment)		88 days
Annualized rate of return		23.68%

Example 35 (10/88)

Macmillan Inc. (MLL - $87 3/4 - NYSE) is in the middle of a takeover battle between KKR and Maxwell communications. KKR has a definitive agreement with the board to acquire the company in a two stepped $90.05 offer. The offer calls for a $90.05 cash tender for 91% of the shares to be followed by a merger consisting of subordinated debentures and warrants with a stated "value" of $90.05.

Maxwell communications has made a competing tender offer of $90.25 for 100% of the shares. The Maxwell offer is conditioned upon the invalidation of certain "lock-up" options granted to KKR by the Macmillan Board. These "lock-ups" have thus far stymied the bidding process. Maxwell is seeking a court action to void the agreements, but has lost the first round. An appeals hearing is scheduled for November 2.

For now we will have to assume we will receive the KKR $90.05 deal. By making a small investment in put options to cover 9% of our position (for the "backend" shares), we can lock in the value of the second step and thus the value of the deal to us. We expect a close by November 25. We will benefit more with a higher price from Maxwell.

The large spread (30% annualized) is indicative of the expected rates of returns that exist today in the arbitrage business. The finite pool of funds in risk arbitrage is being directed away from tail-end type deals such as Macmillan to chase the more exciting prospects of the enormous RJ Nabisco's and the Kraft's that are pending.

MLL	
Front End (90.05 x .91)	$81.95
Backend (85.00 X .09)	7.65
Net Value	89.60
Current Price	$87.75
Cost of Put ($1.50 x .09)	0.135
Plus Commission	0.04
	87.925
Gross Profit	1.675
Gross Profit %	1.91%
Holding Period (expect a November 25 payment)	23 days
Annualized Rate of Return	30.23%

Example 36 (11/88)

Kraft, Inc. (KRA - $102 1/8 - NYSE) has agreed to be acquired by Phillip Morris in a $106.00 per share tender. Excluding the pending RJR Nabisco situation, the Kraft deal is the second largest in takeover history. The tender is scheduled to expire on December 2. Receiving HSR clearance from the FTC remains the final hurdle before consummation. Phillip Morris received a second HSR request from the FTC (a request for more information). Though it is an uncertainty, we do not see any specific business overlap problems and we therefore believe the takeover will ultimately receive governmental approval. We think clearance by December 2 is realistic, but to be conservative, we will assume that it takes until the middle of the month to get such blessing.

KRA	$106.00
Plus Dividend	0.00
Net Value	106.00
Current Price	$102.125
Plus Commission	0.04
	102.165
Gross Profit	3.835
Gross Profit %	3.75%
Holding Period (expect a December 15 payment)	22 days
Annualized Rate of Return	62.28%

Example 37 (12/88)

RJR Nabisco (RJR - $90 1/2 - NYSE) has agreed to be acquired by KKR in a two-stepped LBO with an intended value of $109 per share. We are to receive $109 cash in the front-end tender for 74% of our shares and $109 intended value in two paper issues (a PIK preferred and a PIK convertible debenture) for the back-end shares. In order to eliminate the market risk of the backend shares, we can buy February 80 put options to lock in a value of $76 for 24% of our position. Caution: the risk in this strategy is if the tender gets extended beyond the February option expiration date (February 17), in which case the puts become worthless. Not withstanding that risk, we expect a tender close in early February and payment by February 15.

RJR Front-End ($109 x .74)	$80.66
Back-End ($80 x .26)	20.80
Net Value	101.46
Current Price	$90.50
Cost of Put ($4.00 x .26)	1.04
Plus Commission	0.04
	91.58
Gross Profit	9.88
Gross Profit %	10.79%
Holding Period (expect a February 15 payment)	41 Days
Annualized Rate of Return	96.04%

Example 38 (1/88)

Michigan Energy Resources (MCG - $30 1/8 - NYSE) is in a definitive agreement to be acquired by Utilicorp United, Inc. Shareholders are to receive $22.32 face amount in Utilicorp convertible preferred stock (tentative pricing of 8 7/8%, +15% conversion) and one share of MCG's cable business. We estimate that the cable spinoff will have a trading level of about $11. The merger is subject to the approval of the Michigan Public Service Commission, a tax-free ruling on the cable spinoff by the IRS and on shareholder approval. The tax ruling is not expected before April. The merger itself is not expected to occur until June.

The primary risk is the market risk inherent in our estimation in the trading value of the cable spinoff. The tax ruling is also a concern. Additionally, the illiquidity of the stock gives us the "roach motel" problem; you can check in, but you can't check out, in the event of a deal problem. The expected return is perhaps on the thin side considering the obstacles. Even so, the deal is interesting and one worth monitoring.

MCG	
Conv. Pfd.	$22.32
Cable Spinoff	11.00
Dividend	0.38
Net Value	33.70
Current Price	$30.13
Plus Commission	0.04
	30.17
Gross Profit	3.54
Gross Profit %	11.70%
Holding Period (expect a June 30 payment)	158 days
Annualized Rate of Return	27.03%

Example 39 (2/89)

Texas Eastern Corp. (TET - $50 1/2 - NYSE) is to be acquired by Panhandle Eastern in two-stepped $53 transaction. We are to receive $53 cash in front end tender for 80% of our shares and $53 in Panhandle stock (subject to a collar of $23 to $26) for the remaining 20% in the backend merger. Our primary risks are antitrust, which at most should cause a modest delay, and the trading level of Panhandle as it affects the value of our backend shares. The "market" risk of the backend shares can be eliminated by buying April 50 puts on 20% of our position. In doing so we are locking in a value at the tender expiration, which is the date we calculate our rate of return off of. Assuming a minor delay from HSR, we expect an April 7 payment versus its scheduled March 20 expiration.

TET Front-end ($53 X .80)	$42.40
Back-end ($50 X .20)	10.00
Dividend	0.00
Net Value	$52.40
Current Price	$50.50
Cost of Put ($2.50 x .20)	0.50
Plus Commission	0.04
	51.04
Gross Profit	1.36
Gross Profit %	7.66%
Holding Period (expect an April 7 payment)	32 days
Annualized Rate of Return	30.39%

Example 40 (3/89)

Champion Spark Plug (CHM - $20 3/8 - NYSE) Cooper Industries recently completed its tender offer for all of Champion Spark Plug at $21 per share. For whatever reason, only 83.26% of the outstanding shares were tendered to Cooper. The remaining 16.74% will be taken out in a subsequent merger at the same $21.00. The merger, which requires a proxy to be filed with the SEC and mailed to shareholders should close in early to late June. At $20.375, the expected rate of return is far short of exciting. On the other hand, our only true risk is time, as there is no turning back by Cooper since they already own 83% of the shares. It is conceivable that we could see a two month deal rather than the three months that we are assuming. The return, though modest, is not excessively low considering the risk and considering the alternative investments at hand.

CHM		$21.00
Dividend		0.00
Net Value		21.00
Current Price		$20.375
Plus Commission		0.04
		20.415
Gross Profit		0.585
Gross Profit %		2.87%
Holding Period (expect a June 30 payment)	92 days	65 days
Annualized Rate of Return	11.37%	16.09%

Example 41 (4/89)

Holly Farms Corporation (HFF - $61 3/8 - NYSE), has outstanding a $63.50 tender offer for all of the shares of Holly Farms Corp. Tyson has been doing battle with ConAgra, Inc., the "white knight" suitor for control of Holly over the last several months. Shareholders recently voted down a stock swap merger agreement between ConAgra and Holly valued at about $61. ConAgra still possesses certain lockup options that it was granted as part of the Holly merger agreement. Tyson won a preliminary injunction in Delaware against the lockups. But before it will accept shares in its tender offer, Tyson is insisting on a permanent invalidation of the lockups. Thus far, ConAgra has stubbornly said that is will fight the injunction to the highest court of appeals. It will take an estimated three months to reach the highest level in the Delaware court system.

With two corporate bidders intently interested in a particular property such as Holly, it appears that our probable downside is $63.50 and a lengthy wait in the neighborhood of three months. On the other hand, ConAgra may reconsider its position and work out a monetary settlement with Tyson for dropping the lockups. In this case, we could conceivable see $63.50 in a month or less. Better yet, if ConAgra decides its court battle is futile but really wants to own Holly, it could raise its offer above $63.50, in which case we are back in a bidding war.

HFF		$63.50
Dividend (Est. ex date = 4/26)		0.33
Net Value		63.83
Current Price		$61.375
Plus Commission		0.04
		61.415
Gross Profit		2.415
Gross Profit %		3.93%
Holding Period	30 Days	90 days
Annualized Rate of Return	47.84%	15.95%

Example 42   (5/89)

Thrifty Rent-a-Car (TFTY - $27 3/8 - OTC) has signed a definitive agreement to be acquired by Chrysler Corp. in a $27.75 tender offer. The tender has commenced and is scheduled to expire on June 21. Both Ford and General Motors have been involved as equity players in a few rental car company LBO's over the past year. Since none of these deals encountered any problems with the FTC, we did not expect Chrysler and Thrifty to have an antitrust problem. Financing is not an issue and we expect payment a couple days after the stated expiration.

TFTY	$27.75
Dividend	0.00
Net Value	$27.75
Current Price	$27.375
Plus commission	0.04
	$27.415
Gross Profit	0.335
Gross Profit %	1.22
Holding Period (expect a 6/23/89 payment)	23 days
Annualized rates of return	19.39%

Example 43 (7/89)

Marion Laboratories (MKC - $35 7/8 - NYSE) agreed to be acquired by Dow Chemical in an unusual and complex deal that carries a face value of about $38 per share. In the first step tender, shareholders are to receive $38 cash for at least 38% of their shares. In exchange for their remaining shares, holders will receive a share in the new company, Marion Merrill Dow Inc. The Merrill Dow represents Dow Chemical's drug company, which is being contributed to the new company by Dow. In addition to the one share, we will also get a transferrable right that will pay us the difference between $45.77 and the price of MMD on September 30, 1991 (26 months), but subject to a maximum payment of $15.77. As long as MMD trades above $30 in two years, we are guaranteed $45.77 for our one share plus one right package. If the stock is trading above $45.77, it's all gravy. To arrive at a present value we discount the $45.77 package back 26 months at say 15%. We then weight the frontend tender and the backend by the 38% minimum prorate. There are no apparent regulatory hurdles of substance. The tender should be completed before the end of August.

MKC Frontend ($38 x 0.38)	$14.44
Backend (PV of $45.77 x 0.62)	20.93
Dividend	0.00
Net Value	35.37
Current Price	$34.75
Plus commission	0.04
	$34.79
Gross Profit	0.58
Gross Profit %	1.67%
Holding Period (expect a 8/31 payment)	35 Days
Annualized Rate of Return	17.39%

Example 44 (8/89)

Warner Communications (WCI - $65 1/4 - NYSE) As noted in last month's Background section, Time, Inc. completed the frontend $70 tender for 50% of Warner Communications. For the backend, or merger consideration, shareholders are to receive a package of securities with a "stated value" of $70. On this issue, Warner, Warner's bankers and Time are way out of touch with reality. At least that's a charitable explanation for their calculating a $70 valuation on the following package. Shareholders are to receive $35 face of an 8 3/4% (cash) convertible (at $200) preferred stock, $26 face of an 11%, 4 year PIK, convertible (at $225) preferred stock and Warner's equity interest in BHC. The companies claim that the two converts should trade a little better than face and that the BHC will trade at about $8.30-$8.40 per share of Warner. At the present time we feel reasonably comfortable that the two converts together will trade at their face value. BHC on the other hand, has in our estimation, a trading value of only $5.00, or 50% its private market value of $10.00.

Providing a proxy to shareholders remains the only regulatory obstacle. With a 50% + ownership position in Warner, Time is effectively locked in to completing the merger. Thus no "deal" risk exists. Furthermore, starting August 26, interest at the rate of 9% will accrue on the $70 value until the effective date of the merger, and so our "time" risk is minimal. Our only risk is that the merger securities trade well below our assumed level. Even with the estimated $1.36 of interest that will accrue to us (in the form of additional preferred), the expected return is modest given the market risk. We look for a mid-November close. When-issued trading will commence once the proxy is mailed (in about six weeks).

WCI 8¾% Conv. Pfd.	$35.00
11% Conv. Pfd.	26.00
BHC	5.00
Interest	1.36
Dividend	0.00
Net Value	$67.36
Current Price	$65.25
Plus Commission	0.04
	$65.29
Gross Profit	2.07
Gross Profit %	3.17%
Holding Period (expect a 11/16/89 payment)	77 days
Annualized Rate of Return	15.03%

Example 45 (9/89)

Lin Broadcasting (LINB - $104.00 - OTC) has elected to restructure rather than submit to an "iffy" offer from McCaw. The agreement is Lin's response to McCaw Cellular's $110 hostile tender offer, which remains outstanding. The transaction calls for Lin shareholders to receive $20 cash, one share in Lin's T.V. unit (a spinoff), which we believe will trade at $15 per share, and one share of the a new company to be called Lin Cellular. The new company will combine the cellular interests of Lin with those of Bell South. We estimate Lin Cellular may trade around $70 to so per share. Taken together, we estimate the package is worth $105 - $115.

With two corporate industry players romancing for the same company and a stock price trading 5% below the two offer prices, what more could we ask for? As with most apparent layups, there are a few catches. For starters, the merging of the Lin and Bell South cellular properties may take at least six months to a year because Judge Harold Green (refer to Mobile Communications) must approve the merger (as Bell South is an RBOC). Second, as our valuation range indicates, cellular interests remain fluid. In fact, the Bell South deal gives us considerable 'market exposure. As for the McCaw tender offer, it's not a foregone conclusion that McCaw can generate sufficient financing, especially in light of the current junk bond market problems.

On the other hand, over the next six to twelve months, cellular valuations should increase, and thus so should the trading value of the new company. More importantly, McCaw was recently in talks with LIN to effect a deal worth $127.50/share. If financing is available, we could see another McCaw offer more towards that number. Furthermore, if McCaw does raise its offer, we could find ourselves in the midst of a bidding war. Thus, we are looking at a fairly volatile situation, with market and time risk on the downside (with Bell South) and a potential bidding war on the upside. For now, we will assume we get either one of the two $110 deals, with the difference being timing.

Example 46 (10/89)

Phillips Industries (PHL - $23 5/8 - NYSE), will to be taken private by Merrill Lynch in a $25.50 cash merger (LBO). The merger is conditioned upon shareholder approval and the receipt of sufficient financing to complete the deal. In the current environment, the financing of any LBO is suspect. Accordingly, the spread is relatively large. There are, however, a few compelling reasons why this LBO will get done. For starters, Merrill Lynch intends to invest $150 million in equity in the LBO, or roughly 20% of the purchase price. That level of equity is twice the amount of the typical LBO. Obviously, the higher the equity, the easier a transaction is to finance. Second, based on our analysis, $25.50 is not an overly full price. Finally, the definitive agreement allows for any interested third party bidder to review the books and meet with management.

The proxy should be filed shortly for an end of the year targeted close. We will assume a mid-January, 1990 close.

PHL	$25.50
Dividend	0.15
	25.65
Net Value	
Current Price	$23.625
Plus Commission	0.04
	23.665
Gross Profit	1.985
Gross Profit %	8.4%
Holding Period (expect a 1/15/90 payment)	76 days
Annualized Rate of Return	40.35%

Example 47 (11/89)

North-West Telecommunications (NOWT - $23 5/8 - NASDAQ) has agreed to be acquired by Pacificorp in a $44.13 merger. Ninety percent of the merger consideration will be in the form of Pacificorp stock and the remaining ten percent in cash. The number of Pacificorp shares to be distributed will be determined by an averaging period just prior to the close. Thus our market risk is limited to a few days. In addition to shareholder approval, the merger requires FCC approval as North-West operates local telephone service, cellular telephone systems and a small cable television system. We are told that no PUC (public utility commission) approval is required due to the structure of the deal. An IRS opinion that the transaction is tax-free is also required. Lastly, Pacificorp needs sufficient time to buy enough of its stock in the open market to distribute as the merger consideration (rather than distribute newly issued stock). We should see a July close at the latest, and very likely a mid-May close based on our estimate on how long it will take Pacificorp to cross the various hurdles. With time being the only apparent uncertainty in this transaction, we are satisfied with the modest expected return.

	Worst Case	Likely Case
NOWT	$ 44.13	$ 44.13
Dividend (2)	0.264	0.264
Net Value	44.394	44.394
Current Price	$ 40.50	$ 40.50
Plus Commission	0.04	0.04
	40.54	40.54
Gross Profit	3.854	3.854
Gross Profit %	9.51%	9.51%
Holding Period in days		
(expect a 7/15/90 or 5/15/90 payment)	244	167
Annualized Rate of Return	14.22%	20.78%

Example 48 (12/89)

Great Northern Nekoosa (GNN - $61 1/2 - NYSE) was the subject of a $63 hostile tender offer by Georgia Pacific, which followed GP's original tender of $58. As noted last month, this proposed deal fits into the category of strategic corporate transactions. To date, Great Northern has publicly stated that they are not interested in a merger and would like to carry on as an independent company. Using a number of legal actions, Great Northern has attempted to rid itself of Georgia Pacific through the courts. An antitrust action, which is currently being heard in Connecticut, appears to be their biggest effort. Importantly, Georgia Pacific has already received antitrust clearance from the FTC. Logic says that some 40 lawyers at the FTC reviewed and cleared the proposed combination, a Federal District Judge in Connecticut would most likely agree (though logic does not always hold in a court of law).

In their favor, Great Northern possesses a poison pill, which keeps anyone, including Georgia Pacific, from buying more than 20% of the company. However, the Great Northern Rights Agreement also has a provision that allows shareholders to call a meeting to vote on whether or not to redeem the pill. The meeting has been called and is set for March 20, 1990.

Without a poison pill, without any apparent regulatory problems and with a "real" fully financed corporate buyer, its probable that Great Northern will be taken over. It's more a question of when, at what price and by whom. Its doubtful that we will see a poison pill vote. If Great Northern loses its antitrust action, for example, we may see the company put itself up for sale. To take the conservative outlook we will assume that Great Northern will give in to Georgia.

Example 49 (1/90)

Aristech Chemical (ARS - $25 1/4 - NYSE) In response to an unwanted $25 per share offer from Huntsman Chemical, the management of Aristech Chemical announced that they proposed a $26 buyout with the help of Mitsubishi Corp. As it turned out, what management said and what they are doing is quite different. The real proposal is for the Japanese giant, Mitsubishi Corp. to buy Aristech for $26, and that management will participate in the equity of the new company. Mitsubishi is to provide 85% of the equity and arrange all of the bank financing (a fully financed strategic corporate buyer in drag). The intention is to effect a 45 day tender offer.

Huntsman Chemical has said it wants to bid higher ($27+) but needs more time. Due to the current environment, the market is placing absolutely no overbid, or bidding war premium on the stock. We anticipate a $26 cash tender at the least.

ARS	$26.00
Dividend	0.00
Net Value	26.00
Current Price	$ 25.25
Plus Commission	0.04
	25.29
Gross Profit	0.71
Gross Profit %	2.81%
Holding Period (expect a 3/20/90 payment)	43 days
Annualized Rate of Return	23.83%

Example 50 - GNN Revisited   (2/90)

Great Northern Nekoosa (GNN - $65 3/8 - NYSE) As noted in the Example Update section, Great Northern Nekoosa has agreed to be acquired by Georgia Pacific in a $65.75 tender. We will also receive a $0.33 dividend that goes ex on February 26. Now that the transaction is friendly, there are no longer any legal or other obstacles. The tender is fully financed and scheduled to expire March 6. Given the level of risk, the expected return is tremendous, yet not unusual in the current environment. The spread demonstrates the reduced competition that we face relative to prior periods.

GNN	$ 65.75
Dividend	0.33
Net Value	66.08
Current Price	$65.375
Plus Commission	0.04
	65.415
Gross Profit	0.665
Gross Profit %	1.02%
Holding Period (expect a 3/12/90 payment)	12 days
Annualized Rate of Return	30.92%

Example 51 (3/90)

<u>Rorer Group Inc. (ROR - $67 1/4 - NYSE)</u> Rorer Group Inc. has signed a definitive agreement to merge with Rhone-Poulenc in a two-stepped transaction (which was modeled after the Marion-Dow Chemical combination). In the first step, Rhone-Poulenc is tendering for 50% of the Rorer shares at $78. The second step calls for shareholders to receive one share of the new company (RRP) plus one contingent value right (CVR). Each CVR will entitle the holder to receive the difference below which RRP is trading and $98.26, with a maximum payout of $46.26 in 3 years from RRP (or in the case of 4 years, a guaranteed value of 106.12 with a maximum payout of $54.12). So subject to RRP trading above $52 in three years or four we are assured a value on our backend shares of at least $98.26 (or $106.12). If one gives any credibility to the company's projections that RRP will earn $11.00 per share in four years, we can feel reasonably comfortable with the $52 floor. To be conservative we need to go out in four years, rather than three, and discount back the future expected value of the RRP/CVR package (plus dividends) to the tender expiration at say 15%. Using the prorate figure, we arrive at a blended value of Rorer at the tender expiration (or payment to be exact) date. Prior to the tender expiration, Rorer shareholders must approve the transaction because it is a Pennsylvania corporation. This hurdle calls for a proxy, which will dictate our time frame. We currently anticipate to be paid on the tender by the end of May.

ROR Frontend ($78 x 0.50)	$39.00
Backend (PV of $106.12 x 0.50)	31.25
Dividend	0.37
Net Value	70.62
Current Price	$67.25
Plus Commission	0.04
	67.29
Gross Profit	3.33
Gross Profit %	4.95%
Holding Period (expect a 5/31/90 payment)	62 days
Annualized Rate of Return	29.13%

Example 52 (4/90)

Telecom USA (TTT - $38.00 - NYSE) has agreed to be acquired by MCI Communications in a $42 cash merger. The combination requires numerous regulatory approvals. As with any merger, the FTC must give its antitrust clearance. This proposed marriage combines the #2 (MCI) and the #4 (Telecom) Competitors in the domestic long distance telephone service industry, thus antitrust is an issue. On the other hand, MCI will only be adding an estimated 1½% share to its currently estimated 13% share. Using the technical (or quantitative) guidelines that the government follows (the Herfindahl Index) to determine undue market concentration, the merger shouldn't be considered problematic. Next, MCI must get approval from the 38 states that Telecom does business in. The vast majority of these states will only require a filing. Many, however, will require filings, comment periods, waiting periods and possible hearings. Considering the large number of states in question, the political flavor that these types of state regulatory proceedings often take and the strength of consumer advocacy groups in this country, MCI and Telecom could see any number of snarls or hangups (no pun intended) getting by this hurdle. MCI must also get the FCC's blessing. At the very least, the FCC requires filings to be made and a few comment periods before they will give their approval. If no protests are filed this process should take approximately three months. With protests, the procedure could extend substantially further.

MCI stated that it believes the deal can be closed in four to six months. Given the above, we tend to think it is more likely to see the latter. Considering the potential pitfalls in overcoming the various hurdles, the expected return is not that impressive. At this point we have bought only a small position. As developments unfold and progress is made (or not made) we will reevaluate our position.

TTT	$42.00
Dividend	0.00
Net Value	42.00
Current Price	$38.00
Plus Commission	0.04
	38.04
Gross Profit	3.96
Gross Profit %	10.41%
Holding Period (expect a 10/15/90 payment)	178 Days
Annualized Rate of Return	21.35%

Example 53 (5/90)

Dennison Manufacturing Co. (DSN - $27 3/8 - NYSE) Dennison Manufacturing Co. has agreed to merge with Avery International in a stock swap transaction. Dennison shareholders are to receive 1.12 shares of Avery for every Dennison share owned. As with all mergers, a proxy must be filed with, and cleared by, the SEC. The companies must also receive antitrust (HSR) clearance. It appears to us that this proposed combination poses significant overlap (antitrust) issues in two or more major product lines. Until we get a better handle on a number of items, such as the relevant market definitions in question and if a palatable "fix" exists if the government does ultimately have a problem with the merger, we are not interested in buying more than a token position. This decision is strengthened by the fact that business has been weak at Dennison, and so the downside in the event of no deal, is that much more unquantifiable. Additionally, since this is a stock swap deal it is necessary for us to short Avery in order to lock in the spread (and avoid market risk). A broken deal would typically cause the holder to lose money on both the long (Dennison) and the short (Avery) as arbs scramble to cover their short. For now we will continue our research and monitor the situation.

DSN AVY (26.25) x 1.12	$29.40
Dividend (Net of AVY Div.)	0.17
Short Interest	0.36
Net Value	29.93
Current Price	$27.375
Plus Commission	0.04
	27.415
Gross Profit	2.515
Gross Profit %	9.17%
Holding Period (expect a 10/1/90 payment)	123 Days
Annualized Rate of Return	27.22%

Example 54 (6/90)

Schaefer Value Trust (SAT - $10 1/2 - NYSE) is a closed-end mutual fund that trades on the New York Stock Exchange. In March the fund's management proposed that the trust be liquidated. Shareholders approved the liquidation at the end of May. With the trust trading at a discount to its net asset value, an arbitrage opportunity existed. But since the fund was made up of a basket of stocks, the NAV was not fixed and posed significant market exposure. That had been the case until the final holdings were sold.

As of June 11, the trust was 100% in cash (invested in T-bills) and had an NAV of $10.63. The bulk of the capital was to be distributed by mid-July. With the idle cash earning interest, we anticipated receiving about $10.70 on or about July 15.

SAT (NAV)	$10.63
	0.07
Interest	
Net Value	10.70
Current Price	$10.50
Plus Commission	0.02
	10.52
Gross Profit	0.18
Gross Profit %	1.71%
Holding Period (expect an 7/15/90 payment)	28 Days
Annualized Rate of Return	22.30%

Example 55 (6/90)

Contel Corp. (CTC - $32 3/4 - NYSE) has agreed in principle to merge with GTE Corp. in a stock swap merger. Contel shareholders are to receive 1.27 GTE shares. Once a definitive agreement is reached, the merger will require an "effective" proxy, shareholder approval, PUC approvals of some 30 states and FCC approval. Based on the progress that MCI and Telecom have made in their transaction, it would be reasonable to expect that this deal could be accomplished in approximately six months. We also believe that the deal as structured, is on the low end of the Contel valuation spectrum. A small possibility exists for a higher bid from a third party.

To lock in an acceptable spread we have to short 1.27 shares of GTE for every share of Contel. Given the six month time frame, we can expect to receive two Contel dividends and we can expect to pay out two GTE dividends. We will also receive an interest rebate on the cash from our short GTE shares.

CTC (1.27 x 28 (GTE))	$35.56
CTC Dividend (.275 x 2)	0.55
GTE Dividend (.365 x 2)	(0.73)
Short Interest	0.85
Current Price	$32.75
Plus Commission	0.09
	32.84
Gross Profit	3.39
Gross Profit %	10.32%
Holding Period expect a 1/31/91 payment)	183 Days
Annualized Rate of Return	20.59%

Example 56 (8/90)

Kay Jewelers Inc. (KJI - $12 3/4 - NYSE) has agreed to be acquired by Ratners Group PLC, the British jeweler, in a stock swap merger. Shareholders are to receive a Ratners convertible preferred that is convertible into one Ratners ADR (American Depository Receipt), which equals three shares of Ratners common. The preferred is to pay a $1.20 dividend (after 15% withholding). The companies originally valued the preferred at $17, or an 18% premium over the parity value of the preferred (i. e. the price of one ADR + 18%) . The price of Ratners has since dropped to $12 3/4, and thus assuming the same 18% we arrive at a value of $15 for the preferred. To be conservative we will assume that the market will only pay a 15% premium, or $14.50 for the preferred.

The major hurdle in the deal has already been cleared. Ratners insisted on redeeming the majority of two Kay bond issues at below face-value. Ratners recently purchased about 75% of the larger issue, and thus eliminated the obstacle. In fact, Ratners now has an irrevocable $80 million invested in Kay, which, for all intents and purposes eliminates the risk of nonconsumation. What remains is a fair amount of market risk, which is the major reason for the enormous spread. Downward pressure in Ratners will undoubtedly pull down the trading value of the preferred. However, at $14.50, the preferred will yield over 8%. At 8%, a convertible preferred of such a quality balance sheet is likely to hold its value even with a drop in the underlying common. Nonetheless, in light of the market exposure, our disciplines dictate that we will own only a small to medium size position.
The proxy was filed on July 27, and we expect a mid-October close.

KJI (Ratners Preferred)	$14.50
Dividend	0.00
Net Value	14.50
Current Price	$12.75
Plus Commission	-0.04
	12.79
Gross Profit	1.71
Gross Profit %	13.37%
Holding Period (expect a 10/15/90 payment)	54 Days
Annualized Rate of Return	90.37%

Example 57 (11/90)

<u>DeSoto Inc. (DSO - $42 1/2 - NYSE)</u> as discussed in the Background section, DeSoto Inc. is working through a plan of liquidation. Now that the asset sales have closed and the distributions declared, the vast majority of the risk is out of the stock. Looking forward we have the time value of money and a modest amount of market risk. The market risk comes with the eventual trading value of the detergent business ("NEWCO"). But with a clean balance sheet, projected earnings of a $1.00 per share and an annual dividend of $0.40 per share, a fully distributed trading value (in several months) of say $5.00 is quite conservative.

Because there are three different distributions on three different dates, we need to discount the latter two back at say 25% annualized to the first distribution date in order to arrive at a present value. We will assume the stub trades at about $5.00 nine months from now when the pension surplus is paid out.

DSO	
1st dist.	$24.00
2nd dist. (PV of 11.50 from 12/21)	11.35
3rd dist. (PV of $5 + $4.40 from 8/31/91)	7.90
Net Value	$43.25
Current Price	$42.50
Plus Commission	0.04
	42.54
Gross Profit	0.71
Gross Profit %	1.67%
Holding Period (expect a 12/7/90 payment)	14 Days
Annualized Rate of Return	43.51%

Example 58 (10/90)

<u>VeloBind, Inc. (VBND - $8 3/4 - OTC)</u> is a maker of book binding machines and other office products, agreed to merge with General Binding Corporation. Shareholders are to receive $9.77 cash. The merger is subject to antitrust clearance and shareholder approval. While both companies are in the binding equipment business, they do not actually have any products in direct competition. HSR is scheduled to expire on November 8. The proxy was filed with the SEC on October 1. We look for an early December vote and a late December close (as targeted by General Binding). Again, as with Tony Lama, the one practical problem with the deal is the illiquidity of Velobind and the difficulty in buying a meaningful position.

VBND	$ 9.77
Dividend	0.00
Net Value	$ 9.77
Current Price	$ 8.75
Plus Commission	0.04
	8.79
Gross Profit	0.98
Gross Profit %	11.15%
Holding Period (expect a 12/31/90 payment)	73 Days
Annualized Rate of Return	55.75%

Example 59 (9/90)

Tony Lama Inc. (TLAM - $8 5/8 - OTC) has agreed to be acquired by Justin Industries in a $9.00 cash tender. The tender is fully financed. While both companies, among other things, manufacture cowboy boots, we do not believe there is an antitrust issue. The only potential glitch is that Justin has a dissident shareholder group (owns 12% of Justin) that is trying to block the deal. The litigants claim that Justin management is entrenching itself by buying Tony Lama at a premium price and over-leveraging the balance sheet.

The transaction does not require Justin shareholder approval and thus the dissident action should have no bearing on the Tony Lama tender. The one practical problem with the deal is the illiquidity of Tony Lama and the difficulty in buying a meaningful position.

TLAM	$ 9.00
Dividend	0.00
Net Value	9.00
Current Price	$ 8.625
Plus Commission	.02
	8.645
Gross Profit	0.355
Gross Profit %	4.11%
Holding Period (expect a 10/12/90 payment)	18 Days
Annualized Rate of Return	83.26%

Example 60 (12/90)

MCA Inc. (MCA - $67.00 - NYSE) agreed to be acquired by Matsushita Electric Industrial Co. of Japan in a $66 cash tender. Shareholders will receive 0.20 shares of Red Oak, a newly created holding company that will consist of the WWOR television station. In addition, $0.17 per share in dividends and $0.02 per share from the poison pill redemption will be paid. Prior to consummation, Matsushita and MCA must file an information statement, or Form 10, with the SEC regarding the Red Oak spin-off. They must also get short form approval from the FCC. These hurdles should be completed by early January. The tender should be completed by the middle of January. We value Red Oak at $350 to $400 million, or $4.00 to $4.50 per MCA share on a private market basis. We expect it to trade at approximately 50 cents on the dollar, or a conservative $2.00 per MCA share. WWOR is likely to be attractive to a number of large T.V. station owners. Thus, we may be overly cautious with our estimated trading level as the market may anticipate a merger proposal in the foreseeable future.

MCA	$66.00
Red Oak (0.2 shares)	2.00
Dividend (& PP)	0.19
Net Value	$68.19
Current Price	$67.00
Plus Commission	0.04
	67.04
Gross Profit	1.15
Gross Profit %	1.72%
Holding Period (expect a 1/15/91 payment)	25 Days
Annualized Rate of Return	25.04%

Example 61 (1/91)

Vista Chemical Co. (VC - $52 3/4 - NYSE) agreed to be acquired by RWE AG of Germany in a $55 cash tender. Financing is not an issue as well as Exxon-Florios. Antitrust, on the other hand might be an issue. Apparently, there is an overlap in what is called high purity alumina. The numbers would indicate a fix may be necessary. However, since this product represents less than 5% of Vista's annual revenues, its highly unlikely to be a deal stopper. The real issue is time. Assuming the tender is extended beyond the end of February, we will most likely receive a $0.45 quarterly dividend. To be conservative, we will assume an end of March close.

VC	$55.00
Dividend	0.45
Net Value	$55.45
Current Price	$52.75
Plus commission	0.04
	52.79
Gross Profit	2.66
Gross Profit %	5.04%
Holding Period (expect a 3/31/91 payment)	66 Days
Annualized Rate of Return	27.87%

Example 62 (2/91)

Square D Company (SQD - $76 3/4 - NYSE) has received an unsolicited $78 per share cash merger proposal from Schneider S.A., a large French electrical equipment manufacturer. Financing should not be an issue. It appears to us that there is not a substantial antitrust concern, though a second HSR request is a likely possibility. While the two companies have very similar businesses, Schneider is principally in Europe and Square D is principally in the U.S. The EC commission may also take a look at the transaction on antitrust grounds, but also should not be a problem. In the end, Exxon-Florio should also not be an issue.

Schneider's proposal expires on March 1. By that date one of four things will occur: Square D accepts the proposal, Square D rejects the proposal but decides to put itself up for sale, Square D rejects the proposal and states that it wants to remain independent, or Square D rejects and Schneider gives up and goes away. At this point, the latter is highly unlikely because Schneider has taken certain steps with respect to a proxy fight that indicate it's committed to effecting a transaction. Based on corporate precedent, the most likely scenario is the rejection/independence response. In turn Schneider will commence a hostile tender offer. Square D undoubtedly will try to fight the bid. However, prior to Square D's April 24 annual meeting, they will have to come to terms with Schneider or have their entire Board removed from office. Rather than asking whether a deal will occur, the more accurate question is when and at what price. For the sake of simplicity, we will assume that a friendly deal will occur as advertised, though we are likely to see a higher price and a longer time frame.

SQD	$78.00
Dividend	0.58
Net Value	$78.58
Current Price	$76.75
Plus Commission	0.04
	76.79
Gross Profit	1.79
Gross Profit %	2.33%
Holding Period (expect a 4/15/91 payment)	45 Days
Annualized Rate of Return	18.91%

Example 63 (3/91)

US West NewVector Group Inc. (USWNA - $42 - NASDAQ) has agreed to acquire the remaining shares of its 81% owned cellular telephone subsidiary, US West NewVector, in a $44 stock merger. The agreement follows an initial proposal of 0.95 US West shares, or about $37.50 based on current prices. Since US West already has a controlling interest in NewVector, there are no regulatory hurdles other than to get shareholder approval. The one problem is market risk. Shareholders are to receive $44 in US West stock, but that is subject to a collar. NewVector holders will get no more than 1.14 shares and no less than 1.08 shares (with US West trading at $38 5/8's and $40 3/4's respectively) . As long as US West is trading below the top of the collar, or $40 3/4, a spread can not be effectively locked in by shorting US West, as the number of shares to be delivered is not- assured. If US West were to trade substantially below $38 5/8 then we probably could take the risk of US West appreciating substantially on the flip side lies one of the best risk arb opportunities that exists. If US West were to trade above $40 3/4, we could short 1.08 US West and lock in a spread. If US West were then to trade down prior to the averaging period we would end up getting more shares than we locked in. In other words, we could eliminate our market risk and yet still have upside potential. For now we will watch from the sidelines or own a small position and wait to see if an opportunity arises. The following assumes that a true $44 is received.

USWNA	$44.00
Dividend	0.00
Net Value	$44.00
Current Price	$42.00
Plus Commission	0.04
	42.04
Gross Profit	1.96
Gross Profit %	4.66%
Holding Period (expect a 6/28/91 payment)	88 Days
Annualized Rate of Return	19.34%

Example 64 (4/91)

Avon Products Preferred (AVP PRF - $31 7/8 - NYSE) has called for redemption its redeemable preferred stock. The redemption date is June 3. The required redemption price is $31.75, plus accrued dividends, in the form of cash or stock (at Avon's election). Avon elected to exchange stock. Based on a 10 day averaging period, preferred holders are to receive 0.72 Avon common. A $0.50 dividend will also be received. In order to lock in a spread, we have to sell short .72 Avon common. In addition to the dividend, we will receive a short interest rebate of about $0.25. We will also have to pay out the Avon Common dividend of $0.35. The expected annualized return is not tremendous. But the risk that a "called" security is not ultimately called is diminutive. In fact, the risk/reward shown here is indeed tremendous.

AVP Pfd - AVP (.72 x 44.875)	$32.31
Dividend	0.50
Short Rebate	0.25
Less: AVP Div. (.35 x .72)	(0.25)
Net Value	$32.81
Current Price	$31.875
Plus Commission	0.04
	31.915
Gross Profit	0.895
Gross Profit %	2.80%
Holding Period (expect a 6/3/91 payment)	52 Days
Annualized Rate of Return	19.68%

Example 65 (5/91)

NCR Corp (NCR - $103 3/8 - NYSE) as noted in the Background Section, has agreed to be acquired by AT&T in a $110 stock merger. The number of shares of AT&T to be exchanged for each NCR share is based upon a collar of 2.708 to 3.223. That translates into a trading range of $34.125 and $40.625 for AT&T. If AT&T is above $40.625 during the averaging period (which begins 25 days before the close), our ultimate value will be above $110, and visa versa. The 100% stock deal assumes the SEC grants AT&T "pooling of interest" accounting treatment. If not, the transaction will go to 40% cash, 60% stock, though the ultimate value will be the same either way. In terms of hurdles, we have the SEC accounting decision: and then the proxy. At this stage, the risk of non-consumation is exceptionally low. Our only real concern is market risk (i.e., AT&T falling below the bottom of the collar). For this exercise though, we will assume a $110 value and that the merger will close at the end of August.

NCR	$110.00
Dividend	0.37
Net Value	$110.37
Current Price	$103.375
Plus Commission	0.04
	103.415
Gross Profit	6.955
Gross Profit %	6.73%
Holding Period (expect a 8/30/91 payment)	94 Days
Annualized Rate of Return	26.11%

Example 66 (6/91)

United Artists Entertainment (UAEC'A & 'B - $13 3/4 - OTC) agreed to merge with Tele-Communications Inc., which already owns 54% of the cable company. The agreement calls for both the United Artists Class A and Class B shareholders to receive 1.02 Tele-Communications shares. The transaction is subject to shareholder approval from both companies. Other then getting a proxy filed and cleared by the SEC, there are no regulatory hurdles for Tele-Communications since they already have a controlling interest. The proxy should be filed within a couple of weeks. We expect a September 15 vote and close. To set up a position we short 1.02 Tele-Com shares for each United Artist share.

UAEC'A & B (1.02 TCOMA)	$ 14.28
Dividend	0.00
Short Interest Rebate	0.12
Net Value	$ 14.40
Current Price	$ 13.75
Plus Commission	0.04
	13.79
Gross Profit	0.61
Gross Profit %	4.42%
Holding Period (expect a 9/15/91 payment)	88 Days
Annualized Rate of Return	18.35%

Example 67 (7/91)

Glenmore Distilleries Company (GDSB - $40 7/8 - AMEX) agreed to be acquired by United Distillers, which is a subsidiary of Guinness PLC, in a $42.50 cash merger. Shareholders are also to receive a $0.30 dividend that goes ex on July 30. The insiders, who control Glenmore due to superior voting shares, have in excess of 90% of the vote. Therefore the transaction can occur through a Delaware short form merger, meaning no proxy and no information statement. The only hurdle is HSR. Considering the two companies compete in the same industry, a second request is likely. Based upon the pro-forma market share figures we have seen there ultimately should not be a problem. We would expect the second request to delay the close a month or so beyond the normal 30 day waiting period. Prior to the deal announcement, Glenmore was trading at the $18 per share level. Thus, the downside is significant. That coupled with the stock's illiquidity has led to the rather large spread.

GDSB	$ 42.50
Dividend	0.30
Net Value	$ 42.80
Current Price	$ 40.875
Plus Commission	0.04
	40.915
Gross Profit	1.885
Gross Profit %	4.61%
Holding Period (expect a 9/15/91 payment)	46 Days
Annualized Rate of Return	36.56%

Example 68 (8/91)

On-Line Software Int'l Inc. (OSI - $14 3/8 - NYSE) has announced that it was in talks with Computer Associates to be acquired at $15.75 cash per share. A number of hurdles, such as Board approval, the negotiation of a definitive merger agreement and other standard approvals have to be crossed before the merger is official. The companies indicated specifically that shareholder approval was not a condition of the offer. This means we are likely to see a tender offer rather than just a straight cash merger. Though it is unclear whether further due diligence has to be done by Computer Associates, it is reasonably clear that a deal will in fact occur. This conclusion is based on the fact that the companies are very similar (both in the same area of computer software), that Computer Associates is experienced in this type of acquisition and that Computer Associates has an ample balance sheet to effect the acquisition.

We would expect it to take a few weeks for the definitive to be signed and then a month to complete the tender offer. We are looking at a mid October close.

OSI	$15.75
Dividend	0.00
Net Value	$15.75
Current Price	$14.375
Plus Commission	0.04
	14.415
Gross Profit	1.335
Gross Profit %	9.26%
Holding Period (expect a 10/15/91 payment)	49 Days
Annualized Rate of Return	68.99%

Example 69 (9/91)

Beazer PLC ADR (BZR- $8 1/8 - NYSE) agreed to be acquired by Hanson PLC in a cash and warrant exchange offer. Each Beazer ADR (which is the equivalent to 4 normal shares in London) will receive roughly $6.22 in cash and four Hanson warrants "valued" at $2.32. We will also receive a $0.10 dividend. The warrants have identical features to that of an issue that currently trades in London. As part of the agreement, if the existing warrants trade below the implicit $2.32 value, Beazer shareholders will receive additional warrants to make up the shortfall in value. On the other hand, if the price of Hanson common rises in the interim and thus warrants appreciate in value in the interim, the terms of the deal remain unchanged. We therefore have some upside potential at the same time as our downside is cushioned.

The exchange offer should be completed an about two months. There are no regulatory issues to speak of. The one risk (aside from the market risk associated with the warrants) is currency risk between the pound and the dollar. This issue can be neutralized by simply selling forward contracts for the pound (the equivalent amount for $8.50 per share). There is a cost to selling the forward contracts (about $0.08 per share), but it's well worth the haircut to eliminate a potential big risk.

BZR	Cash	$6.22
	Warrants	2.32
Dividend		0.10
Net Value		$ 8.64
Current Price		$8.125
Plus Commission		0.04
Plus Forward Contract		0.07
		$ 8.235
Gross Profit		0.405
Gross Profit %		4.92%
Holding Period (expect an 11/31/91 payment)		61 Days
Annualized Rate of Return		29.43%

142

Example 70 (10/91)

Metro Mobile CTS (MMZB - $21 1/8 - AMEX) has agreed to be acquired by Bell Atlantic in a stock swap merger. The agreement is a bit odd because there is not a specific price per share being offered to Metro Mobile shareholders. Bell Atlantic is buying the company based on a formula that gives a specific value per cellular "pop", adds the value of certain miscellaneous assets that are to be sold and subtracts the debt and interim interest expense that Metro Mobile has and will occur. What we are left with is approximately $24.40 per Metro Mobile share. Shareholders are to receive the formula based value in the form of Bell Atlantic shares, subject to a collar ($45.90 to $50.72). With Bell Atlantic trading just below the bottom of the collar, it is difficult to hedge the position by shorting Bell Atlantic. With a 5.5% plus dividend yield, we are cautiously comfortable staying unhedged with our position. However, with even this level of market exposure, we are unwilling to take on much more than a 25% to 30% of a full position. If Bell Atlantic got near the top of the collar, we would change this assessment.

Bell Atlantic needs an effective proxy, FCC approval, a few state approvals and the infamous Judge Greene's approval. We expect a close in early April 1992.

MMZB	$24.40
Dividend	0.00
Net Value	24.40
Current Price	$21.125
Plus Commission	0.04
	21.165
Gross Profit	3.24
Gross Profit %	15.30%
Holding Period (expect a 4/10/92 payment)	161 days
Annualized Rate of Return	24.63%

Example 71 (11/91)

American Television & Communications Corp. (ATCMA - $53 1/8 - OTC) Time Warner has offered to acquire the remaining public shares of American Television & Communications Corp. Time already owns 82%. The initial proposal calls for ATC shareholders to receive a new Time preferred stock that is convertible (0.4 TWX shares), exchangeable, redeemable and puttable, but pays no dividend. With the conversion feature so far out of money, the preferred will trade principally on its put feature. Three years from the date of issuance holders can put their preferred back to Time for a consideration worth $75 (in cash, stock, or new issue). Thus, the preferred will trade like a three-year zero coupon bond. With such a short time frame the preferred should trade with a fairly tight spread, though the issuer's option of offering "Paper" has chilled some investor appetites. In order to move forward with its offer Time needs ATC's independent Board member approval (though shareholder approval is assured with its 82% vote). Herein lies the reason that this is a very interesting situation. The analysis done by our research staff indicates that ATC is presently worth considerably more than the present value of $75 three years out. Very often a majority owner will make an initial low ball bid in order to make the sweetened final price more palatable. And even if that doesn't happen we will still be compensated by the offer on the table. The transaction will require franchise transfer approval from scores of municipalities because the offer is part of a broader transaction involving a partnership with two Japanese companies (Toshiba and C. Itoh). The transaction is not expected to conclude until the end of May 1992. To value the existing offer we determine where the new preferred will trade once the merger is done. To do that we discount $75 back three years at, say 10%. Again, one note of caution is that Time has the ability to issue a new piece of paper in three years and "claim" its worth $75. Hopefully that option will be negotiated out of the deal.

ATCMA ($75 back three years at 10%)	$56.34
Dividend	0.00
Net Value	$56.34
Current Price	$53.125
Plus Commission	0.040
	$53.165
Gross Profit	3.175
Gross Profit %	5.970%
Holding Period (expect a 5/31/92 payment)	176 days
Annualized Rate of Return	12.39%

Example 72 (12/91)

Sanford Corp. (SANF - $39.00 - OTC) has agreed to merge with Newell Co. in a $40 stock swap merger subject to a collar. The collar is from 1.0 to 0.93 Newell shares, or in other words from $40 to $43 on Newell. In spite of a small overlap in Newell's office product business, there are no regulatory issues to be concerned about. The proxy was filed December 13, and we can expect a close in late February. What makes this situation particularly interesting is that Newell is trading just above the top of the collar. We can set up a modest "worst case" spread while giving ourselves the possibility to earn a substantial return in the event Newell drops to the bottom of the collar in the weeks prior to the close of the merger. If we short Newell at $43.25 and Newell is at $40 during the averaging period our deal value increases to $43.00 from $40. If Newell rises well above $43.25 then we still earn our worst case spread.

	Worst	Best
SANF	40.22	43.25
Dividend (Net of Short Div.)	(0.08)	(0.08)
Short Interest Rebate	0.19	0.19
Net Value	40.33	43.36
Current Price	$39.00	$39.00
Plus Commission	0.04	0.04
	$39.04	$39.04
Gross Profit	1.29	4.32
Gross Profit %	3.30%	11.06%
Holding Period (expect 2/28/91)	57 Days	57 Days
Annualized Rate of Return	21.16%	70.86%

Example 73 (1/92)

Revco 13.125% Sr. Sub Notes ($38 - OTC) After entering Chapter 11 over three years ago, Revco D.S. (the drugstore chain) is on the verge of emerging from bankruptcy through a merger plan with Jack Eckerd Corp. After a reasonably intense bidding process, which also included separate proposals from management, a creditors group and Rite Aid, it appears that Eckerd has sufficient support from the various bondholder, bank and trade creditor groups to have its plan confirmed in bankruptcy court. Each creditor faction is receiving a mixture of cash and debt and equity securities of the new combined company. The 13.125% senior subordinated notes are being offered (per $1,000 face) $70.50 cash plus 0.7912 of a new LYON (liquid yield option note). The LYON is essentially a convertible (into 20.73 common shares), zero coupon bond that's puttable to the company at a specific price and date. In this case the put price is $743.6 in 5 years. The LYON can be valued on a yield to put basis or on a premium to conversion parity basis. Since Jack Eckerd is still a private company (to go public in May) we will use the yield to put method at say 12%.

The remaining hurdles include Eckerd getting a revised disclosure document through the SEC and then mailed to bondholders. We then get a "confirmation hearing" (tentative March 11) and vote. The vote is a much more significant event than in the case of your typical merger. All of the various factions must agree (2/3's vote) . We anticipate that the transaction can be completed by the end of March.

REVCO 13.125%	Cash	$7.05
	LYON	33.38
Interest		0.00
Net Value		40.43
Current Price		$38.000
Plus Commission		0.125
		38.125
Gross Profit		2.305
Gross Profit %		0.605%
Holding Period (expect 3/31/92)		55 days
Annualized Rate of Return		40.12%

Example 74 (2/92)

Salem Carpet Mill, Inc. (SLCR - $8 5/8 - OTC) has agreed to merge with Shaw Industries. Both companies compete in the broadloom carpet business, with Shaw being the industry's largest. Salem shareholders are to receive a minimum of 0.1814 Shaw shares (top of the collar). Holders also have the option to take $7.98 cash for up to half of their shares. With Shaw at $49.125 (well above the collar), that is merely an academic option. By shorting Shaw we can lock in an acceptable spread. Because of the collar we have created an out of the money synthetic put on Shaw. With Shaw so far over the top of the collar ($44) this put will more than likely go away worthless (but you never know). As with most mergers of competitors, this transaction will receive some antitrust scrutiny. We do not see an insurmountable problem. We would expect a close by the middle of May.

SLCR ($49.125 x 0.1814)	$8.91
Dividend	0.02
Negative Dividend	(0.06)
Short Rebate	.06
Net Value	8.93
Current Price	$8.625
Plus Commission	.01
	8.635
Gross Profit	0.295
Gross Profit %	3.42%
Holding Period (expect 5/15/92)	72 days
Annualized Rate of Return	17.32%

Example 75 (3/92)

Grace Energy Corp. (GEG - $17 1/4 - NYSE) As noted in the Background section, W.R. Grace is proposing to acquire the public shares of Grace Energy at $16.50 cash per share. We also noted that the price of $16.50 appears to be well below what would be considered a fair value. Listed below is the breakdown of what we feel is a fair value. The methodologies differ depending on the asset in question. While we do not necessarily believe that Grace will pay full value, we do believe an improvement towards that number will be necessary in order to garner a fairness opinion.

Asset	Methodology	$ mil	Per Share (24.6M)
Gracc Drilling	168 rigs x $.4 mm/rig	67.20	2.74
Offshore	8 rigs x $6.0 mm/rig	48.00	1.95
Homeo-Services	6 x EBDIT ($32.96)	197.74	8.05
Grace Petroleum	$3.00/boe x 43mm bbI	130.00	5.29
Coal	4 x EBDIT of $40 mil	160.00	6.51
Storage Tank	$9 per Barrel of Capacity	53.10	2.16
		656.04	26.70
Debt		(175.00)	(7.12)
Cash		26.00	1.06
		507.04	20.64

Example 76 (4/92)

Alpha Industries (AHA - $3 1/2 - AMEX) received an unsolicited proposal from M/A Con to be acquired in a $4.00 per cash merger. Alpha rebuffed M/A-Com. M/A-Com in turn made the proposal public. This pressure tactic is commonly known as a "bear hug". M/A Con has placed a deadline of May 7 on the offer. Based on their response to date, its likely that Alpha will continue to resist. M/A-Com however, has given every indication that it will take whatever action is necessary in order to accomplish its goal. The fact that M/A-Com has hired a major investment banker and law firm adds credence to this expectation. Financing is not an issue, as M/A-Com has sufficient cash on its balance sheet. The only area that gives us a little pause is antitrust. Certain of their product lines have few U.S. competitors other than each other. But Japan, Inc. is also a major player and the products themselves (semiconductor and microwave components) can be considered commodity in nature. While HSR could add time to the process, we do not think it will be a major hurdle. While the overall size of the transaction is small, we have a motivated buyer and a spread to the offer on the table. We expect ultimately to get a bump in the price. For now we will assume a $4.00 price and a four month time frame, although the latter is also open ended.

AHA	$4.00
Dividend	0.00
Net Value	$4.00
Current Price	$ 3.50
Plus Commission	0.04
	$3.54
Gross Profit	0.46
Gross Profit %	12.99%
Holding Period (expect a 8/31/92 payment)	192 days
Annualized Rate of Return	24.70%

Example 77 (5/92)

Pinelands Inc. (PL - $17 3/4 - NYSE) Pinelands Inc. agreed to be acquired by Chris-Craft Industries in an $18.00 cash tender. The merger will require FCC approval prior to the completion of the tender offer. As a result, the tender could take anywhere from two to six months. In the event no protests are filed with the FCC, we are looking at the shorter time frame. Based on precedent, the probability that not even a nuisance protest is submitted is quite low. We are more than likely looking at a time frame of about five months. As part of the agreement, Chris-Craft has agreed to pay interest at the annual rate of 6% on the $18 after 60 days has passed. With a five month deal we can expect to receive three months of interest, or an additional $0.27. Financing, antitrust and even the FCC (since Chris-Craft is already a T.V. licensee) are non-issues, other than time in the case of the latter. The chances of non-consummation are minimal. While our expected annualized rate of return is indeed modest, we are positioned to earn a substantial return in the event a third party (such as Disney) makes a competing bid.

PL	$18.00
Interest	0.27
Dividend	0.00
Poison Pill Redemption	0.01
Net Value	$18.28
Current Price	$17.75
Plus commission	0.01
	$17.76
Gross Profit	0.52
Gross Profit %	2.93%
Holding Period (expect a 10/12/92 payment)	157 days
Annualized Rate of Return	6.81%

Example 78 (6/92)

Arctic Alaska Fisheries (ICE - $11 1/2 - NYSE) has agreed to be acquired by Tyson Foods in a stock and cash merger. Shareholders are to receive 0.5686 Tyson shares and $2.23 in cash per share. Arctic Alaska is one of the nation's largest harvesters and processors of fish in the northwest. Tyson, while currently the nation's largest chicken producer and processor, is not in the fish processing business. Thus, antitrust should not be an issue. Since this is primarily a stock deal, financing is also not an issue. Based on our experience with Holly Farms a few years ago, Tyson is a quality buyer. The companies are targeting October 5, 1992 for the closing date.

ICE	Stock	(0.5686 x 17.25)	$9.81
	Cash		2.23
Short Rebate			0.05
Dividend			0.00
Poison Pill Redemption			0.01
Net Value			$12.10
Current Price			$11.50
Plus Commission			0.04
			11.54
Gross Profit			0.56
Gross Profit %			4.85%
Holding Period (expect a 10/05/92 payment)			98 days
Annualized Rate of Return			18.07%

Example 79 (7/92)

Nicolet Instrument (NIC - $20 3/4 - NYSE) has signed a definitive agreement to be acquired by Thermo Instrument Systems in a $21 cash tender. The agreement follows several months of discussions between the two companies (including a 13D filing by Thermo). While both companies manufacture analytical instruments, there is little, if any, product overlap. Thus, antitrust is not an issue. Financing is also a non-issue as Thermo's parent (Thermo Electron) is providing financing from its balance sheet. The tender has begun and has an expiration of August 20. We expect to get paid by August 26. The expected return reflects our lower interest rate environment.

NIC	$21.00
Dividend	0.00
Poison Pill Redemption	0.01
Net Value	$21.01
Current Price	$20.75
Plus Commission	0.04
	$20.79
Gross Profit	0.22
Gross Profit %	1.06%
Holding Period (expect a 8/26/92 payment)	26 days
Annualized Rate of Return	14.86%

Example 80 (8/92)

Horizon Carpet (HRZN - $14 5/8 - OTC) agreed to be acquired by Mohawk Carpet in a $15 cash and stock merger. Shareholders will receive about $10.75 in cash and $4.25 worth of Mohawk common. The mixture could change if the trading value of Mohawk appreciates from its current level. The actual amount of shares to be received will be based on an averaging period just prior to the close. Thus, there's no need for us to short Mohawk at this point. The merger itself is quite similar to a transaction this year involving Shaw Industries and Salem Carpet (Example #73). As with the Salem merger, we do not see an antitrust issue. Additionally, financing is not a condition of the agreement (we note that a bank agreement has been arranged). The merger itself offers the buyer economies of scale and Horizon has made a good showing financially for the last several quarters. The only material condition is the satisfaction of environmental due diligence of the Horizon manufacturing facilities. We have been informed that Horizon had an environmental audit done three years ago and was given a clean bill of health. Neither side expects a problem. The proxy was filed August 12. We anticipate a late October close.

HRZN	Cash	10.75
	Stock	4.25
Dividend		0.00
Poison Pill Redemption		0.00
Net Value		15.00
Current Price		$14.625
Plus Commission		0.040
		14.665
Gross Profit		0.335
Gross Profit %		2.28%
Holding Period (expect 10/31/92 payment)		58 days
Annualized Rate of Return		14.37%

Example 81 (9/92)

MidSouth Corporation (MSRR - $19.00 - OTC) agreed to be acquired by Kansas City Southern in a $20.50 cash merger. Kansas City is a Class 1 railroad carrier and MidSouth is a Class 2 carrier. The two railroad concerns have no common customers (shippers) and have almost entirely complimentary lines. Thus, it is doubtful that the merger will be stopped on regulatory grounds. On the other hand, the companies must still go through the regulatory process of the ICC. This process creates our biggest uncertainty; timing. In the best scenario, Kansas City is granted an exemption from the ICC, in which case the merger could be accomplished in 3 1/2 months. The worst case is that the ICC insists on a full blown review, which could take in the neighborhood of 12 months. Based on discussions with the ICC and the companies, a 6 to 8 month time frame is the best guess for this merger. Financing should not be an issue, nor should labor, which often plays a role in rail mergers. For now we will assume an 8 month time-frame, which ultimately should prove conservative. A 6 month time frame improves the annualized return to about 15.5%.

MSRR	$20.50
Dividend	0.00
Poison Pill Redemption	0.00
Net Value	20.50
Current Price	$19.00
Plus commission	0.040
	19.04
Gross Profit	1.46
Gross Profit %	7.67%
Holding Period (expect a 5/29/92 payment)	244 days
Annualized Rate of Return	11.47%

Example 82 (10/92)

Applied Biosystems Inc. (ABIO - $19 3/4 - OTC) agreed to be acquired by Perkin-Elmer Corp. in a stock swap merger. Shareholders are to receive 0.678 shares of Perkin in the swap. Though both companies are in the analytical instrument business, the combination will be purely complimentary (no directly competing products). Thus antitrust should not be a problem. Perkin is a financially strong-quality buyer. Applied shareholders also have some protection against a big negative move in the price of Perkin. If Perkin is trading below $26 1/2 at the time of the vote, Applied Bio has the right to terminate, unless Perkin improves the swap ratio to assure holders a minimum value of $18 per share. Perkin however, has the right to terminate the deal if its environmental due diligence of Applied Bio turns up any major surprises. Perkin has 45 days to complete the audit. Based on conversations with management, we should not see a problem. We expect a late January close.

ABIO ($30.375 x 0.678)	$20.60
Dividend	0.00
Poison Pill Redemption	0.00
Net Value	20.60
Current Price	$19.75
Plus commission	0.040
	19.79
Gross Profit	0.81
Gross Profit %	4.09%
Holding Period (expect a 1/31/92 payment)	91 days
Annualized Rate of Return	16.42%

Example 83 (2/93)

Alden Press Company - signed a definitive agreement to be acquired by APC Holdings (a company formed by Kohlberg Kravis Roberts & Co.) in a $15 cash tender. The tender is subject to financing, regulatory approval, and approval of 50% of the Alden shares outstanding. Financing should not be an issue because of the resources of KKR. Hart-Scott-Rodino should also not be an issue. Even though KKR has a subsidiary in a similar business, World Color Press Inc., the two business do not compete directly and the industry is fragmented. The tender is scheduled to expire on February 26. We expect to get paid March 3.

ALDN	$15.000
Dividend	0.000
Net Value	$15.000
Current Price	$14.875
Commission	0.000
	$14.875
Gross Profit	0.125
Gross Profit %	0.84%
Holding Period (expect a 3/3/93 payment)	23 days
Annualized Rate of Return	13.33%

Example 84 (2/93)

Dahlberg Inc. (DAHL - $22 7/8 - OTC), the maker of the Miracle Ear, received a proposal to be purchased by Bausch & Lomb for $24 cash. Like many of the new deals we have seen, this is a strategic acquisition for Bausch & Lomb. Through Dahlberg, Bausch & Lomb will be acquiring a distribution network for its own hearing aid Sound Choice. Antitrust does not appear to be a concern since Sound Choice is a new product for Bausch & Lomb that is yet to be distributed nationally. Financing is not an issue as Bausch & Lomb has over $400 million of cash on its balance sheet, more than enough to pay for the entire acquisition. Due diligence is essentially complete. We are currently waiting for the signing of the definitive agreement, which should be signed by the end March. The deal is expected to close by June 30, 1993.

DAHL	$24.00
Dividend	0.06
Poison Pill Redemption	0.00
Net Value	24.06
Current Price	$22.875
Plus commission	0.020
	22.86
Gross Profit	1.20
Gross Profit %	5.25%
Holding Period (expect a 6/30/93 payment)	117 days
Annualized Rate of Return	16.38%

Example 85 (4/93)

Katy Industries (KT - $25 1/8 - NYSE) signed a definitive agreement to be acquired by the Carroll family for $25.75 cash per share. The Carroll Family originally proposed to purchase the remaining shares it does not already own for $22 per share in September of 1992 (the Carroll family currently owns 52% of Katy's shares). We see little deal risk given that the buyer is a majority holder and financing is not a condition. The deal is expected to close by June 15, 1993.

KT	$25.75
Dividend	0.00
Poison Pill Redemption	0.00
Net Value	25.75
Current Price	$25.125
Plus Commission	0.025
	25.15
Gross Profit	.60
Gross Profit %	2.39%
Holding Period (expect a 6/15/93 payment)	69 days
Annualized Rate of Return	12.62%

Example 86 (5/93)

Meca Software (MECA - $11 1/4 - OTC) has agreed to be acquired by Chipsoft through a cash tender offer at $11.625. Both Meca and Chipsoft market software for personal income tax preparation. While the Justice Department has stated that it will review this transaction, we believe it will ultimately clear Hart-Scott-Rodino. Defining market shares on the most narrow basis, the combined entity will control a major portion of the software market for personal income tax preparation. This market is an infant market with annual revenues of under $100 million, no barrier to entry, and does not include the personal income tax preparation market serviced by H&R Block. To note, Microsoft's Money program is able to do tax estimates but does not have the ability to print the actual tax forms. In addition, the Business Tax preparation software market is a much larger market at about five time the size of the personal market. The tender offer is set to expire on May 12, 1993. While the company is still hopeful it can clear Hart-Scott-Rodino before then, we believe they will have to extend the tender. To be conservative, we are assuming a June 30, 1993 close.

MECA	$11.625
Dividend	0.000
Poison Pill Redemption	0.000
Net Value	11.625
Current Price	$11.250
Plus Commission	0.025
	11.275
Gross Profit	.350
Gross Profit %	3.10%
Holding Period (expect a 6/30/93 payment)	49 days
Annualized Rate of Return	23.10%

Example 87 (6/93)

Price Stern Sloan Publishing (PSSP - 9 3/8 - OTC) signed a definitive agreement to be acquired by Putnam Berkley, a unit of MCA, in a $9.625 cash tender offer. The offer is conditioned upon 90% of Price Stern's shares being tendered. Holders owning 30% of Price Stern have agreed to the merger. The offer is scheduled to expire June 21, 1993.

PSSP	$9.625
Dividend	0.000
Poison Pill Redemption	0.000
Net Value	9.625
Current Price	$9.375
Plus Transaction Costs	0.025
	9.400
Gross Profit	.225
Gross Profit %	2.39%
Holding Period (expect a 6/21/93 payment)	21 days
Annualized Rate of Return	41.60%

Example 88 (7/93)

Goody-Products (GOOD - $22 1/2 - OTC) entered into an agreement in principle to be acquired by Newell Co. for $24.74 per share in cash. A definitive agreement is subject to due diligence, which is expected to be completed by mid July. Newell has held an equity position in Goody for about three years and increased their position to 13% last year. In addition, both Newell and Goody sell to the same customers (WalMart & Kmart). Thus, Newell knows this company. Antitrust is not a problem, since their products do not overlap.

Goody Products Stock	$24.75
Dividend	.05
Poison Pill Redemption	.00
Net Expected Proceeds	24.80
Current Price	$22.75
Plus Transaction Costs	0.03
	22.78
Gross Profit	2.02
Gross Profit %	8.89%
Holding Period (expect a 10/30/93 payment)	121 days
Annualized Rate of Return	26.8%

Example 89 (8/93)

North American National Corp. (NAMC - $14 1/8 - OTC) North American National signed a definitive agreement to be acquired by Liberty Corp in a $14.75 cash merger. Liberty initially offered $15.25 per share, but lowered the price after the completion of due diligence. We do not anticipate an antitrust problem since North American's pre-need life insurance subsidiary is in contiguous territory to Liberty's. Regulatory approval from the states of Colorado and Ohio is required. Liberty has received a favorable response from these states. Closing is expected by the end of October.

North American National Stock	$14.75
Dividend	.00
Poison Pill Redemption	.00
Net Expected Proceeds	14.75
Current Price	$14.125
Plus Transaction Costs	0.025
	14.15
Gross Profit	.60
Gross Profit %	4.2%
Holding Period (expect a 10/30/93 payment)	87 days
Annualized Rate of Return	17.8%

Example 90 (9/93)

Amoskeag (AMOS - $39.00 - OTC) agreed to be acquired by Fieldcrest Cannon (FLD-$23½ -NYSE) in a $40 cash tender offer. Amoskeag owns supervoting stock in Fieldcrest, representing about 30% of the equity and 80% of the vote of Fieldcrest. Fieldcrest was the victor of an auction process that involved three other bidders, including a higher nominal offer from Springs Industries. The tender offer is subject to the sale by Fieldcrest of a convertible preferred and is set to expire October 15, 1993.

Amoskeag Stock	$40.00
Dividend	.00
Poison Pill Redemption	.00
Net Expected Proceeds	40.00
Current Price	$39.000
Plus Transaction Costs	0.025
	39.03
Gross Profit	.97
Gross Profit %	2.48%
Holding Period (expect a 10/15/93 payment)	45 days
Annualized Rate of Return	20.2%

Example 91 (10/93)

Primerica Corp. (PA - $48.00 - NYSE) signed a definitive agreement with Travelers Corp. (TIC - $37⅞ - NYSE) where in PA will purchase the remaining shares it does not already own for .80423 of PA per TIC share. In addition to antitrust clearance, Primerica needs regulatory approval from the state of Connecticut due to Travelers insurance operations. Given Primerica's 27% ownership in Travelers, we expect the regulatory process to be relatively smooth and swift and anticipate a January 15, 1994 close.

Travelers Stock	$38.60
Net Dividends + Short Interest	.59
Poison Pill Redemption	.00
Net Expected Proceeds	39.19
Primerica Sold Short x .80423	$37.63
Plus Transaction Costs	0.05
	37.68
Gross Profit	1.51
Gross Profit %	4.0%
Holding Period (expect a 1/15/94 payment)	101 days
Annualized Rate of Return	14.5%

Example 92 (11/93)

Celutel (CLU - $7 3/8 - NYSE) signed a definitive agreement to be acquired by Century Telephone for $8 per share, consisting of $4 cash per share plus $4 in Century Telephone Stock, subject to a collar of $27 - $33. Thus, Celutel shareholders will not receive more than .148 shares nor less than .121 shares of Century Telephone. Century Telephone has completed its due diligence and has also received antitrust clearance to complete the transaction. We anticipate a December 31, 1993 closing.

Celutel Stock	$ 8.00
Net Dividends	.00
Poison Pill Redemption	.00
Net Expected Proceeds	8.00
Current	$ 7.38
Plus Transaction Costs	0.03
	7.41
Gross Profit	.59
Gross Profit %	8.0%
Holding Period (expect a 12/31/93 payment)	59 days
Annualized Rate of Return	49.3%

Example 93 (12/93)

Kaufman & Broad Home Corp. (KBS- $18 7/8 -NYSE) will tender for the 5.1 million shares of its special common shares outstanding at $19 per share. There is no financing condition. In addition, there are no regulatory hurdles. The tender is set to expire December 7, 1993.

Kaufman & Broad stock	$19.00
Net Dividends	.00
Poison Pill Redemption	.00
Net Expected Proceeds	19.00
Current	$18.875
Plus Transaction Costs	0.025
	18.90
Gross Profit	.10
Gross Profit %	.53%
Holding Period (expect a 12/10/93 payment)	5 days
Annualized Rate of Return	38.6%

Example 94 (1/94)

Pacific Telesis Group (PAC - $54 1/4 - NYSE), the Regional Bell Operating Company in California, is spinning off its cellular subsidiary Pactel Corp. (PTW - $24 ⅜ - NYSE). PAC sold to the public a 14% interest in PTW at $23 in December. Shareholders of PAC will receive one share of PTW per share of PAC owned. Purchasing one share of Pactel at $54 1/4 and shorting one share of PTW at 24 3/8, creates Pactel Proforma for the spinoff at $29.125 including dividends and short interest. Since PAC proforma will maintain its dividend of $2.18 per share, it will be trading with a dividend yield of 7.5% and 10.4x our internal research staff's earnings per share estimate for 1994 of $2.80. In addition, our research staff believes, PAC proforma should trade at $35 with a dividend yield of 6.2%. We expect the spinoff to occur April 30, 1994, which will be before the auction for personal communications licenses (PCS) in May.

Pacific Telesis - Proforma	$35.00
Pactel Corp (PTW NYSE)	24.38
Net Dividends & Short Interest	.75
Poison Pill Redemption	.00
Net Expected Proceeds	60.13
Current	$54.25
Plus Transaction Costs	0.05
	54.30
Gross Profit	5.83
Gross Profit %	10.7%
Holding Period (expect a 4/30/94 payment)	112 days
Annualized Rate of Return	35.0%

Example 95 (2/94)

Radiation Systems (RADS - $17 1/2 - OTC) signed a definitive agreement to be acquired by Comsat (CQ - $26 3/8 -NYSE) for $18.25 per share in CQ stock subject to a collar of $23 3/8 to $28 5/8 on CQ stock. RADS shareholders will receive no more than .780 shares of CQ nor less than .638 shares of CQ. Comsat at $26 3/8 is near the top of the collar. For every point Comsat trades above $28 5/8, RADS shareholders will receive $0.65 in addition to the $18 1/4. The termination fee on the deal is $7.5 million and CQ has received an option to purchase 15% of RADS at $18.25. In addition, CQ purchased 4.9% of RADS before signing the definitive agreement. The transaction is expected to close May 15, 1994.

Radiation Systems	$18.250
Net Dividends & Short Interest	.025
Poison Pill Redemption	.000
Net Expected Proceeds	18.275
Current	$17.500
Plus Transaction Costs	0.025
	17.575
Gross Profit	.700
Gross Profit %	4.0%
Holding Period (expect a 5/15/94 payment)	97 days
Annualized Rate of Return	15.1%

Example 96 (3/94)

Eldec (ELDC - $12 3/4 - OTC) signed a definitive agreement to be acquired by Crane Co. through a $13 per share cash tender offer. The tender is not conditioned upon financing and antitrust is also not a concern. The withdrawal and expiration of the tender is March 17, 1994. We expect to receive payment by March 21, 1994.

Eldec	$13.000
Net Dividends & Short Interest	.000
Poison Pill Redemption	.000
Net Expected Proceeds	13.000
Current	$12.750
Plus Transaction Costs	0.025
	12.775
Gross Profit	.225
Gross Profit %	1.8%
Holding Period (expect a 3/21/94 payment)	13 days
Annualized Rate of Return	49.5%

Example 97 (4/94)

Grumman Corp. (GQ - $61 3/4 - NYSE) has signed a definitive agreement to be acquired by Northrop for $62 per share through a cash tender offer. Grumman had originally agreed to be acquired by Martin Marietta for $55 per share and Northrop topped that bid with a $60 offer. We initiated a large position to make a return on the Martin Marietta deal and increased the position once it was disclosed that Northrop had previously talked with Grumman concerning a combination between the two companies. While Grumman closed the month at $64 5/8 on speculation that Marietta would top Northrop's bid, the stock has since traded down to $61 3/4. We continue to hold a position to make a return on the $62 tender by Northrop which expires April 15, 1994.

GQ	$62.000
Net Dividends & Short Interest	.000
Poison Pill Redemption	.000
Net Expected Proceeds	62.000
Current	$61.750
Plus Transaction Costs	0.025
	61.775
Gross Profit	.225
Gross Profit %	.4%
Holding Period (expect a 4/18/94 payment)	4 days
Annualized Rate of Return	33.2%

Example 98   (5/94)

RHI Entertainment (RHE - $35 5/8 - NYSE) agreed to be acquired by Hallmark Cards through a $36 per share cash tender offer. The tender is subject to a minimum condition of 66.1% of the shares being tendered and RHI's president and CEO staying on board with the combined company. The tender is not subject to financing and antitrust does not appear to be a problem. The withdrawal and expiration of the tender is May 26, 1994.

RHE	$36.000
Net Dividends & Short Interest	.000
Poison Pill Redemption	.000
Net Expected Proceeds	36.000
Current	$35.625
Plus Transaction Costs	0.025
	35.650
Gross Profit	.350
Gross Profit %	.98%
Holding Period (expect a 5/30/94 payment)	21 days
Annualized Rate of Return	17.0%

Example 99   (7/94)

Lincoln Foodservice (LINN - $15 1/8 - OTC) signed a definitive agreement to be acquired by Welbilt Corp. for $15.60 cash. LINN announced in February that it had received a proposal and conducted an auction. The Welbilt transaction is not subject to financing, due diligence has been completed, and antitrust does not appear to be a problem since there is virtually no product overlap.   The companies anticipate filing a proxy statement within a week. While they believe the transaction can be completed by late August, we are using September 15, 1994 as a closing date to be conservative.

LINN	$15.600
Net Dividends & Short Interest	.000
Poison Pill Redemption	.000
Net Expected Proceeds	15.600
Current	$15.125
Plus Transaction Costs	0.025
	15.145
Gross Profit	.455
Gross Profit %	3.00%
Holding Period (expect a 9/15/94 payment)	63 Days
Rate of Return	17.41%

Example 100 (8/94)

Nature Food Centres (NAFD - $11 3/4 - OTC) signed a definitive agreement to be acquired by General Nutrition Companies through a $12 per share cash tender offer. The tender is subject to at least two thirds of the shares outstanding being validly tendered. The transaction is not subject to financing. The withdrawal and expiration date of the tender offer is August 24, 1994.

NAFD	$12.000
Net Dividends & Short Interest	.000
Poison Pill Redemption	.000
Net Expected Proceeds	12.000
Current	$11.750
Plus Transaction Costs	0.025
	11.775
Gross Profit	.225
Gross Profit %	1.91%
Holding Period (expect a 8/26/94 payment)	18 Days
Rate of Return	38.74%

Example 101 (9/94)

Neutrogena (NGNA - $34 7/8 - OTC) signed a definitive agreement to be acquired by Johnson & Johnson (JNJ - 50 1/2 -NYSE) through a $35.25 per share cash tender offer. The tender is subject to at least two thirds of the shares outstanding being validly tendered. The transaction is not subject to financing. The withdrawal and expiration date of the tender offer is September 23, 1994.

NGNA	$35.250
Net Dividends & Short Interest	.000
Poison Pill Redemption	.000
Net Expected Proceeds	35.250
Current	$34.875
Plus Transaction Costs	0.025
	34.900
Gross Profit	.350
Gross Profit %	1.00%
Holding Period (expect a 8/27/94 payment)	19 Days
Rate of Return	19.26%

Example 102 (10/94)

American Income Holding (AIH - $34 1/4 - NYSE) signed a definitive agreement to be acquired by Torchmark Corp. (TMK- $43 1/2 -NYSE) through a $35 per share cash tender offer. The merger and tender offer have been approved by the directors of AIH, who have received a fairness opinion from Fox-Pitt Kelton Inc. The merger agreement provides that if it is terminated, AIH will pay TMK a fee of $12 million plus expenses. The transaction has received early termination under HSR. While the tender offer expiration is October 19, we anticipate an extension due to the deal being subject to Indiana and Texas state insurance regulatory boards. We expect the deal to close before the end of the year. We have accumulated a large position.

AIH	$35.000
Net Dividends & Short Interest	.000
Poison Pill Redemption	.000
Net Expected Proceeds	35.000
Current	$34.250
Plus Transaction Costs	0.025
	34.275
Gross Profit	.725
Gross Profit %	2.12%
Holding Period (expect a 11/15/94 payment)	39 days
Annualized Rate of Return	19.8%

Example 103 (11/94)

Purolator Products (PFIL - $24 3/4 - OTC) signed a definitive agreement to be acquired by Mark IV Industries (IV-$21 1/4-NYSE) through a $25 cash tender offer. Mark IV currently owns 4.7% of PFIL and has offered to purchase the remaining shares outstanding. The tender offer has been approved by PFIL's board and the HSR antitrust waiting period has expired. The offer and withdrawal rights of the tender will expire on November 4. We have a large position.

PFIL	$25.000
Net Dividends & Short Interest	.000
Poison Pill Redemption	.000
Net Expected Proceeds	25.000
Current	$24.750
Plus Transaction Costs	0.025
	24.775
Gross Profit	.225
Gross Profit %	.91%
Holding Period (expect a 11/10/94 payment)	20 days
Annualized Rate of Return	16.6%

Example 104 (12/94)

Triconex Corp. (TCNX - $17 1/2 - OTC) agreed to be acquired by Siebe PLC through a $17.75 cash tender offer. TCNX's board has unanimously approved the offer. The offer is conditioned upon a majority of TCNX being tendered and Exxon-Florio approval. Siebe is entitled to a $2.4 million fee if the deal is terminated. Siebe's offer resulted from an auction process conducted by Smith Barney beginning in June of this year. A number of process control companies looked at TCNX, however Siebe emerged as the only serious bidder. We have established a position.

TCNX	$17.750
Net Dividends & Short Interest	.000
Poison Pill Redemption	.000
Net Expected Proceeds	17.750
Current	$17.500
Plus Transaction Costs	0.025
	17.525
Gross Profit	.225
Gross Profit %	1.28%
Holding Period (expect a 12/23/94 payment)	14 days
Annualized Rate of Return	33.47%

Example 105 (1/95)

Caesars World Inc.(CAW - $66 3/4 - NYSE) signed a definitive agreement to be acquired by ITT Corp. (ITT-$86 7/8-NYSE) through a $67.50 cash tender offer. ITT needs the approval of regulators in Nevada, New Jersey, and Canada to consummate the merger. These approvals are expected by February 1st. ITT is also discussing potential problems the merger might create with the NBA and NHL. (ITT is buying the N.Y. Knicks and N.Y. Rangers from Viacom.) Their league policies prohibit franchise owners from having an interest in a sports-betting operation. (CAW runs the largest sports book in Las Vegas.) ITT anticipates all issues in this regard will be resolved promptly. The CAW acquisition would be a major boost to ITT's plan to become a forceful presence in entertainment-related industries. We have a large position in CAW.

CAW	$67.500
Net Dividends & Short Interest	.000
Poison Pill Redemption	.000
Net Expected Proceeds	67.500
Current	$66.750
Plus Transaction Costs	0.025
	66.775
Gross Profit	.725
Gross Profit %	1.09%
Holding Period (expect a 02/06/95 payment)	19 days
Annualized Rate of Return	20.86%

Example 106 (2/95)

Pyramid Technology (PYRD - $15 3/4 - OTC) entered into a definitive merger agreement with Siemens Nixdorf. Siemens will acquire the PYRD shares it doesn't already own in a $16 cash tender offer. (Siemens currently owns more than 17% of PYRD and has a warrant to acquire an additional 7%.) The offer is subject to a 51% minimum tender condition, HSR, and Exxon-Florio approvals. The offer and withdrawal of the tender expire on February 24. We have established a position in PYRD.

PYRD	$16.000
Net Dividends & Short Interest	.000
Poison Pill Redemption	.000
Net Expected Proceeds	16.000
Current	$15.750
Plus Transaction Costs	0.025
	15.775
Gross Profit	.225
Gross Profit %	1.42%
Holding Period (expect a 03/01/95 payment)	21 days
Annualized Rate of Return	24.79%

Example 107 (3/95)

Club Car Inc. (CLBC - $24 7/8 - OTC) signed a definitive agreement to be acquired by Clark Equipment Co. (CKL-$52 7/8-NYSE) through a $25 cash tender offer. CLBC is one of the largest makers of golf carts in the world with a roughly 35% share of the U.S. market for golf carts. CKL reached an agreement with holders of about 28% of CLBC's stock, including Kelso & Co. fund affiliates, who have agreed to tender to the company. CLBC went public last October at $17 1/2. The withdrawal and expiration of the tender is March 8. We have established a position.

CLBC	$25.000
Net Dividends & Short Interest	.000
Poison Pill Redemption	.000
Net Expected Proceeds	25.000
Current	$24.875
Plus Transaction Costs	0.025
	24.900
Gross Profit	.100
Gross Profit %	.40%
Holding Period (expect a 03/13/95 payment)	5 days
Annualized Rate of Return	29.32%

Example 108 (4/95)

Chicago and North Western Transportation Company (CNW - $34 3/4 - NYSE) agreed to be acquired by Union Pacific Corporation (UNP-$55 1/2-NYSE) through a $35 cash tender offer. UNP already owns 30% of CNW and is buying the 70% of CNW it doesn't own for $1.2 billion. The Interstate Commerce Commission has given UNP approval to convert its non-voting stock into voting shares, and further approval to merge the two railroads is unnecessary. Freight railroads, which have been reporting strong earnings from a rising U.S. economy and market-share gains, have been prowling for mergers as they strive to compete with rival truckers. The withdrawal and expiration of the tender is April 19, 1995. We have established a large position.

CNW	$35.000
Net Dividends & Short Interest	.000
Poison Pill Redemption	.000
Net Expected Proceeds	35.000
Current	$34.750
Plus Transaction Costs	0.025
	34.775
Gross Profit	.225
Gross Profit %	.64%
Holding Period (expect a 04/21/95 payment)	14 days
Annualized Rate of Return	16.87%

Example 109 (5/95)

E-Systems Inc. (ESY - $63 3/4 - NYSE) agreed to be acquired by Raytheon Corp. (RTN - $72 1/2-NYSE) for $64 per share in cash or $2.3 billion. The tender offer is subject to RTN's receipt of a majority of ESY's shares and HSR approval. The offer expires April 28. RTN received financing commitments from Chemical Bank, Bank of America, and Chase Manhattan Bank to provide up to $3 billion in unsecured credit for the tender offer. A termination fee of $75 million would be payable to RTN in the event that a third party bidder emerges. ESY is a major producer of advanced electronic systems for defense markets with a primary focus on high-tech intelligence and reconnaissance equipment. RTN is a leader in air defense missile and radar systems and other military electronics products, as well as in major household appliances. We have established a position in ESY.

ESY	$64.000
Net Dividends & Short Interest	.000
Poison Pill Redemption	.000
Net Expected Proceeds	64.000
Current (Purchase on April 6, 1995)	$63.625
Plus Transaction Costs	0.025
	63.650
Gross Profit	.35
Gross Profit %	.55%
Holding Period (expect a 05/03/95 payment)	20 days
Annualized Rate of Return	10.04%

Example 110 (7/95)

Marion Merrell Dow (MKC - $25 1/2 - NYSE) announced that the FTC approved the pending sale of Dow Chemical's (DOW-$71 3/8-NYSE) interest in MKC to Hoescht AG. Hoescht will acquire all of MKC for $25.75 per share or about $7.1 billion. The sale of MKC to Hoescht has now been approved by the European Union and other necessary regulatory agencies. In addition, MKC received final approval from the SEC for an information statement which will soon be mailed to all of MKC's public shareholders. An MKC shareholder meeting will be held on July 18 to approve the transaction. We will receive a $0.25 a share dividend for the second quarter. We are also entitled to a prorated dividend for the third quarter, depending on when the merger is closed. We hold a position in MKC.

MKC	$25.750
Net Dividends & Short Interest	.300
Poison Pill Redemption	.000
Net Expected Proceeds	26.050
Current (Purchase on June 26, 1995)	$25.500
Plus Transaction Costs	0.025
	25.525
Gross Profit	.525
Gross Profit %	2.06%
Holding Period (expect a 08/01/95 payment)	33 days
Annualized Rate of Return	22.75%

Example 111 (6/95)

CRSS Inc. (CRX - $14 1/2 - NYSE) entered into a merger agreement with American Tractabel Corporation (ATC). The agreement provides for ATC to acquire CRX through a $14.50 cash tender offer, to be followed by a cash merger at the same price for shares not tendered. The offer is subject to a majority tender condition and HSR approval. CRX is a leading developer and operator of independent power and industrial energy facilities. CRX's energy projects represent a total capital investment of approximately $823 million. ATC is also a leading owner, operator and developer of independent power generation projects in the United States and Canada. We have a position in CRX.

CRX	$14.500
Net Dividends & Short Interest	.000
Poison Pill Redemption	.000
Net Expected Proceeds	14.500
Current (Purchase on May 17, 1995)	$14.250
Plus Transaction Costs	0.025
	14.275
Gross Profit	.225
Gross Profit %	1.58%
Holding Period (expect a 06/20/95 payment)	27 days
Annualized Rate of Return	21.31%

Example 112 (8/95)

Automotive Industries Holdings (AIHI - $33 1/8 - OTC) signed a definitive agreement to be acquired by Lear Seating (LEA-$27-NYSE) through a $33.50 cash tender offer. The offer is conditioned upon, among other things, the tender of a majority of the shares outstanding, HSR antitrust clearance and the receipt by Lear of sufficient financing for the acquisition. Lear has obtained a commitment letter from Chemical Bank to provide the necessary funding for the acquisition. The withdrawal and expiration of the tender is August 16, 1995. We have established a position in AIHI.

AIHI	$33.500
Net Dividends & Short Interest	.000
Poison Pill Redemption	.000
Net Expected Proceeds	33.500
Current (Purchase on July 19, 1995)	$33.060
Plus Transaction Costs	0.025
	33.085
Gross Profit	.415
Gross Profit %	1.25%
Holding Period (expect a 08/18/95 payment)	25 days
Annualized Rate of Return	18.31%

Example 113 (10/95)

Ren Corp. (RENL - $19 13/16 - OTC) agreed to be acquired by Gambro AB for $20 per share, or $180 million, sweetening its previous offer. Gambro already owns 53% of RENL. On July 14, Gambro offered to acquire the rest of RENL for $18 per share. RENL's board formed an independent committee to review that offer. Gambro then raised the offer by $2 a share to seal the deal. Gambro will acquire the remaining RENL shares through a $20 cash tender offer. RENL is a leading provider of dialysis services. Gambro makes equipment used for dialysis, cardiac surgery and blood separation. The withdrawal and expiation of the tender is October 17, 1995. We have a position in RENL.

RENL	$20.000
Net Dividends & Short Interest	.000
Poison Pill Redemption	.000
Net Expected Proceeds	$20.000
Current	$19.8125
Plus Transaction Costs	0.0250
	$19.8375
Gross Profit	.163
Gross Profit %	.82 %
Holding Period (expect a 10/20/95 payment)	16 days
Annualized Rate of Return	18.71 %

Example 114 (11/95)

CBS Inc. (CBS - $80 1/2 - NYSE) announced it would hold a special meeting of CBS shareholders on November 16 to vote on Westinghouse Electric Corp.'s (WX - $13 3/4 - NYSE) $5.4 billion acquisition offer. WX is offering $81 per share in cash plus interest accreted at a 6% annual rate from September 1, 1995. WX stated it expects to receive FCC approval for the deal in November. Thus, it is conceivable that all the requisite approvals could be in place by the end of November. We hold a large position in CBS.

CBS	$81.000
Net Dividends & Interest	1.220
Poison Pill Redemption	.000
Net Expected Proceeds	$82.220
Current	$80.500
Plus Transaction Costs	0.025
	$80.525
Gross Profit	1.695
Gross Profit %	2.10%
Holding Period (expect a12/15/95 payment)	40 days
Annualized Rate of Return	19.21%

Example 115 (1/96)

CBI Industries, Inc. (CBI - $32 7/8 - NYSE) and Praxair, Inc. (PX - $33 7/8 - NYSE) announced the signing of a definitive merger agreement, in which PX will acquire all of CBI's shares outstanding for a price of $33 per share. The Boards of both companies have unanimously approved the agreement. PX will amend its tender offer, commenced on November 3, by increasing the offer price to $33. The offer will be subject to a 51% minimum tender condition and HSR approval. PX also stated it had reached a tentative agreement with the Federal Trade Commission staff concerning a settlement and consent order. This agreement indicates that the HSR tender condition is likely to be satisfied promptly. PX also stated that it intends to sell CBI's oil terminal and engineering subsidiaries after it completes the acquisition. We have a position in CBI.

CBI	$33.000
Net Dividends & Short Interest	.000
Poison Pill Redemption	.000
Net Expected Proceeds	$33.000
Current (Purchase on December 27, 1995)	$32.750
Plus Transaction Costs	0.025
	$32.775
Gross Profit	.225
Gross Profit %	.69%
Holding Period (expect a 01/19/96 payment)	17 days
Annualized Rate of Return	14.74%

Example 116 (2/96)

Tivoli Systems Inc. (TIVS - $47 1/16 - OTC) and IBM Corporation (IBM - $108 1/4 - NYSE) announced the signing of a definitive merger agreement under which IBM has commenced a cash tender offer for TIVS' shares at $47.50 per share. TIVS is a leading provider of systems management software and services for client / server networks. The merger will combine TIVS' advanced client / server technology with IBM's host-based systems management products. Together the companies hope to provide customers with the most comprehensive, open systems management solutions for network-centric computing. The tender offer is subject to a 51% minimum tender condition and HSR clearance. The withdrawal and expiration of the tender is March 1, 1996. We have a position in TIVS.

TIVS	$47.500
Net Dividends & Short Interest	.000
Poison Pill Redemption	.000
Net Expected Proceeds	$47.500
Current	$47.0625
Plus Transaction Costs	0.000
	$47.0625
Gross Profit	.4375
Gross Profit %	.93%
Holding Period (expect a 03/05/95 payment)	29 days
Annualized Rate of Return	11.70%

Example 117 (2/94)

Duracraft Corp. (DUCR - $43 1/4 - OTC) signed a definitive agreement to be acquired by Honeywell, Inc. (HON-$51 7/8-NYSE) through a $43.50 cash tender offer. Southborough, Massachusetts-based DUCR is the nation's biggest maker of fans, heaters, humidifiers, and air cleaners. The company will become part of Honeywell's home and building controls unit, which produces thermostats and air cleaners. The offer is conditioned upon two-thirds of DUCR's outstanding shares being tendered as well as anti-trust clearance. The offer is not subject to financing. In connection with the transaction, Bernard Chiu, DUCR's Chairman and CEO, has agreed to tender his 31 percent position in DUCR. The withdrawal and expiration of the tender is March 15 , 1996. We have established a position in DUCR.

DUCR	$43.500
Net Dividends & Short Interest	.000
Poison Pill Redemption	.000
Net Expected Proceeds	$43.500
Current	$43.250
Plus Transaction Costs	0.025
	$43.275
Gross Profit	.225
Gross Profit %	.52%
Holding Period (expect a 03/19/95 payment)	13 days
Annualized Rate of Return	14.6%

Example 118 (3/96)

MediSense Inc. (MSNS - $44 9/16 - OTC) signed a definitive agreement to be acquired by Abott Laboratories (ABT-$41 3/4-NYSE) for about $876 million, or $45 pe share, giving ABT a foothold in the glucose-monitoring market. Based in Waltham, Massachusetts, MSNS is the world's fourth-largest maker of glucose self-testing systems for people with diabetes. Under terms of the agreement, ABT will commence a cash tender offer on April 4, 1996. The transaction is subject to regulatory and other customary approvals. The withdrawal and expiration of the tender is May 1, 1996. We have established a position in MSNS.

MSNS	$45.000
Net Dividends & Short Interest	.000
Poison Pill Redemption	.000
Net Expected Proceeds	$45.000
Current	$44.5625
Plus Transaction Costs	0.000
	$44.5625
Gross Profit	.4375
Gross Profit %	.98%
Holding Period (expect a 05/03/96 payment)	29 days
Annualized Rate of Return	12.35%

Example 119 (4/96)

Cornerstone Natural Gas, Inc. (CGA - $5 7/8 - ASE) signed a definitive agreement to be acquired by El Paso Energy Corp. (EPG-$36-NYSE) through a $6 cash tender offer. CGA has 700 miles of pipelines and seven natural gas processing facilities in East Texas and Louisiana that handle 250 million cubic feet of gas per day. The company also markets natural gas and natural gas liquids. Holders of more than 50 percent of CGA's fully diluted outstanding shares have granted El Paso Energy options to purchase all shares of CGA common stock, as well as options and warrants held by them. The withdrawal and expiration of the tender is May 24, 1996. We have a position in CGA.

CGA	$6.000
Net Dividends & Short Interest	.000
Poison Pill Redemption	.000
Net Expected Proceeds	$6.000
Current	$5.875
Plus Transaction Costs	0.025
	$5.900
Gross Profit	.235
Gross Profit %	1.69%
Holding Period (expect a 05/28/96 payment)	25 days
Annualized Rate of Return	24.7%

Example 120 (5/96)

Micom Communications Corp. (MICM - $11 7/8 - OTC) signed a definitive agreement to be acquired by Northern Telecom Ltd. (NT-$54 1/2-NYSE) through a $12 cash tender. MICM, a Semi Valley, California based network software company, has struggled during the past two years with inventory problems at the company and among its customers. For two consecutive years, the company said its third-quarter earnings would fall short of expectations. Odyssey Partners L.P. and other MICM shareholders have agreed to tender 5.15 million shares, or 44 percent of MICM's total. The transaction is subject to a majority of MICM's share being tendered as well as antitrust clearance. The withdrawal and expiration of the tender is June 14, 1996. We have established a position in MICM.

MICM	$12.000
Net Dividends & Short Interest	.000
Poison Pill Redemption	.000
Net Expected Proceeds	$12.000
Current	$11.875
Plus Transaction Costs	0.015
	$11.890
Gross Profit	.11
Gross Profit %	.93%
Holding Period (expect a 06/18/96 payment)	13 days
Annualized Rate of Return	25.98%

Example 121 (7/96)

Community Health Systems (CYH - $51 3/4 - NYSE) signed a definitive agreement to be acquired by Forstmann Little & Co. through a $52 cash tender offer. The investment firm, which buys companies to sell later for a profit, will acquire the chain of 38 hospitals in 18 states for a total of $1.37 billion including debt. New York-based Forstmann will invest $1 billion of its own funds in the purchase and Chase Manhattan agreed to provide $900 million in bank financing. After refinancing and share repurchases, the transaction will provide CYH with about $500 million to buy more hospitals. The transaction is subject to Forstmann Little receiving a majority of CYH's 19.7 million shares outstanding during the tender offer. The withdrawal and expiration of the tender offer is July 9, 1996. We have established a position in CYH.

CYH	$52.000
Net Dividends &: Short Interest	.000
Poison Pill Redemption	.000
Net Expected Proceeds	$52.000
Current	$51.750
Plus Transaction Costs	0.025
	$51.775
Gross Profit	.225
Gross Profit %	.43%
Holding Period (expect a 07/12/96 payment)	7 days
Annualized Rate of Return	22.67%

Example 122 (7/96)

AMBAR Inc. (AMBR - $17 13/16 - OTC) signed a definitive agreement to be acquired by The Beacon Group Energy Investment Fund, L.P. through a $18 cash tender offer. In connection with the agreement, Beacon has also entered into an agreement to purchase the 51% of AMBR's shares currently owned by Randolph M. Moity, the company's Chairman, President and Chief Executive Officer, and the 6% of AMBR's shares owned by Kenneth J. Bouttee, an AMBR director. The tender offer is subject to various conditions, including that at least 90% of the company's outstanding shares are tendered. AMBR designs, blends and markets certain fluids and chemicals, and provides environmental services, primarily along the Louisiana and Texas Gulf Coast. The withdrawal and expiration of the tender offer is August 15, 1996. We have a position in AMBR.

AMBR	$18.000
Net Dividends & Short Interest	.000
Poison Pill Redemption	.000
Net Expected Proceeds	$18.000
Current	$17.813
Plus Transaction Costs	0.020
	$17.833
Gross Profit	0.167
Gross Profit %	0.93%
Holding Period (expect a 08/12/96 payment)	7 days
Annualized Rate of Return	48.9%

Example 123 (8/96)

Orchard Supply Hardware Stores Corp. (ORH - $34 3/4 - NYSE) signed a definitive agreement to be acquired by Sears, Roebuck and Co. (S-$43 3/4-NYSE) through a $35 cash tender offer. ORH's 61 hardware superstores in California will help Sears carve a niche between Home Depot's cavernous stores and mom-and-pop shops. The 115 Sears hardware stores and ORH focus on homeowners needing small repairs. Freeman Spogli & Co. acquired ORH in May 1989 and the company completed its initial public offering in March 1989. In connection with the acquisition agreement, Freeman Spogli, which is ORH's largest shareholder, has agreed to tender their 1,604,043 shares, and have also granted Sears an option on such shares at $35.00 per share, which can be exercised under certain circumstances. ORH received a fairness opinion from Montgomery Securities. The transaction is conditional on a majority of ORH shares being tendered as well as antitrust clearance. The withdrawal and expiration of the tender is September 18, 1996. We have established a position in ORH.

ORH	$35.000
Net Dividends & Short Interest	.000
Poison Pill Redemption	.000
Net Expected Proceeds	35.000
Current	$34.750
Plus Transaction Costs	0.025
	34.775
Gross Profit	0.225
Gross Profit %	0.65%
Holding Period (expect a 08/20/96 payment)	15 days
Annualized Rate of Return	15.74%

Example 124 (9/96)

Duracell International (DUR - $64.00 - NYSE) agreed to be acquired by Gillette Co. (G-$72 3/8-NYSE) through a $7 1/2 billion stock swap. The purchase would enable G to reduce its reliance on shaving products and expand its own consumer-products family, which already includes Right Guard and Foamy toiletries, Parker pens and Oral-B toothbrushes. DUR would in turn get to exploit the massive advertising and distribution muscle that G has in markets worldwide. Under terms of the agreement, G will exchange 0.904 of a share for each one held by DUR shareholders, and assume $575 million in debt. Based on a G closing price of $72 3/8, it would value DUR at about $65.43 per share. G will issue 108 million shares and take a charge of about $275 million. Kohlberg Kravis & Roberts Co., which owns 41.1 million DUR shares, representing 34 percent of DUR's outstanding shares, has agreed to vote in favor of the merger. The transaction is expected to close in mid-December. We have established a hedged position in DUR.

DUR (0.904 Gillette)	$65.427
Net Dividends & Short Interest	.640
Poison Pill Redemption	.000
Net Value	$66.067
Current	$64.000
Plus Transaction Costs	0.040
	$64.040
Gross Profit	2.027
Gross Profit %	3.16%
Holding Period (expect 12/30/96)	90 days
Annualized Rate of Return	12.84%

Example 125 (10/96)

Big B, Inc. (BIGB - $17 1/8 - OTC) signed a definitive agreement to be acquired by Revco D.S. (RXR-$31 3/4-NYSE) for $17.25 a share, or $380 million, putting an end to RXR's two month long hostile tender offer for BIGB. BIGB had rejected an earlier bid of $15 per share from the No.2 drugstore chain, saying it was too low. BIGB's board unanimously approved the higher bid and recommended that shareholders accept it. BIGB, the 10th largest drugstore chain, also dropped its "poison pill" anti-takeover measure, and both RXR and BIGB dropped all litigation that stemmed from the earlier bid. RXR will benefit from the larger presence in the Southeast as well as efficiencies created by the combination of stores covering a wider area. BIGB adds 397 stores in the Southeastern U.S. to RXR's 2,200 stores in 14 Midwestern, Southeastern and Eastern states. RXR extended its tender offer to November 15 from October 25. We have a position in BIGB.

BIGB	$17.250
Net Dividends & Short Interest	.000
Poison Pill Redemption	.000
Net Expected Proceeds	$17.250
Current	$17.125
Plus Transaction Costs	0.000
	$17.125
Gross Profit	.125
Gross Profit %	.73%
Holding Period (expect a 11/18/96 payment	14 days
Annualized Rate of Return	19.04%

Example 126 (11/96)

Edmark Corp. (EDMK - $15 3/8 - OTC) signed a definitive agreement to be acquired by International Business Machines Corp. (IBM-$159 3/8-NYSE) through a $15.50 per share cash tender offer. The acquisition would give IBM a library of education software for children from kindergarten through grade 12. IBM has said it plans acquisitions in the software markets to shore up its offerings. In September, it agreed to buy insurance software maker Professional Data, and earlier this year, it bought Tivoli Systems Inc. for $743 million. The tender offer is conditional on acceptance by holders of at least two-thirds of EDMK's outstanding shares. Antitrust clearance has already been obtained. The withdrawal and expiration of the tender offer is November 16, 1996. We have established a position in EDMK.

EDMK	$15.50
Net Dividends & Short Interest	.00
Poison Pill Redemption	.00
Net Expected Proceeds	15.50
Current	$15.375
Plus Transaction Costs	0.015
	15.39
Gross Profit	0.11
Gross Profit %	0.71%
Holding Period (expect a12/18/96 payment)	14 days
Annualized Rate of Return	18.63%

Example 127 (12/96)

Tylan General (TYGN - $15 13/16 - OTC) signed a definitive agreement to be acquired by Millipore Corp. (MIL-$41 3/8-NYSE) through a $16.00 per share cash tender offer. TYGN is a supplier to the microelectronics industry of precision mass flow controllers, pressure and vacuum measurement and control equipment and ultraclean gas panels. The sale would strengthen MIL's position in the market for equipment used in the making of biotech drugs and semiconductor equipment. The news ends four months of speculation over a possible sale of TYGN. In August, the company said it received offers and retained Goldman, Sachs & Co. to evaluate potential buyers. The offer is conditioned on MIL receiving a majority of TYGN's outstanding shares in the tender and has cleared antitrust review. The withdrawal and expiration of the tender is January 21, 1997. We have established a position in TYGN.

TYGN	$16.00
Net Dividends & Short Interest	.00
Poison Pill Redemption	.00
Net Expected Proceeds	16.00
Current	$15.812
Plus Transaction Costs	0.015
	15.827
Gross Profit	0.17
Gross Profit %	1.07%
Holding Period (expect a 01/23/97 payment)	17 days
Annualized Rate of Return	23.06%

172

Example 128 (2/97)

Innotech, Inc. (IIII - $13 5/8 - OTC) signed a definitive agreement to be acquired by Johnson & Johnson Inc. (JNJ-$60 5/8-NYSE) through a $13.75 cash tender offer. IIII is a Roanoke, VA-based company which develops, manufactures and sells lens products, desktop lens casting systems and related consumables that enable eye care professionals and optical retailers to custom fabricate high quality prescription eyeglass lenses at the point of sale. IIII has approximately 9 million shares outstanding. The offer is subject to the purchase of a majority of the outstanding shares of IIII. Antitrust approvals have already been obtained. The withdrawal and expiration of the tender offer is March 17, 1997. We have established a large position in IIII.

IIII	$15.750
Net Dividends & Short Interest	.000
Poison Pill Redemption	.000
Net Expected Proceeds	15.750
Current	$15.625
Plus Transaction Costs	0.015
	15.640
Gross Profit	.11
Gross Profit %	.70%
Holding Period (expect a 03/19/97 payment)	15 days
Annualized Rate of Return	17.11%

Example 129 (3/97)

TPC Corp. (TPC - $13 1/4 - NYSE) signed a definitive agreement to be acquired by PacificCorp (PPW-$21 1/8-NYSE) for $288 million in cash, adding a company that sells natural gas to utilities in the Midwest and East to one of the largest electric companies in the western U.S. Under terms of the agreement, PPW has commenced a $13.41 cash tender offer to purchase all outstanding shares of TPC. Buying TPC will let PPW store and sell natural gas in the Midwest and East. Improved technology and rising supplies have made burning natural gas one of the least-expensive ways of making electricity. PPW is one of six electric utilities that have announced plans to buy a natural gas company in the last year. Because TPC is not an interstate pipeline company, PPW won't face the regulatory obstacles that other utilities have in acquiring natural gas assets. The transaction has received antitrust approval and is conditional on PPW receiving a majority of TPC shares in the tender offer. The withdrawal and expiration of the offer is April 14, 1997. We have established a position in TPC.

TPC	$13.410
Net Dividends & Short Interest	.000
Poison Pill Redemption	.000
Net Expected Proceeds	$13.410
Current	$13.250
Plus Transaction Costs	0.025
	$13.275
Gross Profit	$0.135
Gross Profit %	1.02%
Holding Period (expect a 04/16/97 payment)	14 days
Annualized Rate of Return	26.5%

Example 130 (5/97)

Fibreboard Corp. (FBD - $54 3/8 - ASE) signed a definitive agreement to be acquired by Owens Corning (OWC-$42 5/8-NYSE) through a $55 cash tender offer. OWC will pay a total $640 million in cash and assumed debt for the maker of vinyl siding, in a move that would strengthen OWC's position in one of the fastest-growing parts of the building materials industry. FBD, which had sales of $469 million last year, markets its products, including manufactured stone, through its own network of distributors who sell mainly to builders and remodeling contractors. OWC makes glass-fiber insulation, roofing and other building materials that it sells through independent distributors who sell mainly to builders and remodeling contractors. OWC said it isn't worried about litigation FBD faces for injuries caused by the exposure to asbestos. FBD is seeking a so-called global settlement under which its insurers would fund a trust to pay the claims. A U.S. court affirmed the global settlement in July 1996, but opponents have filed an appeal with the U.S. Supreme Court. If the Supreme Court overturns the Fifth Circuit Court's decision, the insurers have agreed to settle all claims made up until August 27, 1993, and up to $2 billion plus interest in claims filed against FBD after that. OWC is confident this would cover FBD's liability. The withdrawal and expiration of the tender is June 26, 1997. We have established a position in FBD.

FBD	$55.000
Net Dividends & Short Interest	.000
Poison Pill Redemption	.000
Net Expected Proceeds	$55.000
Current	$54.375
Plus Transaction Costs	0.025
	$54.400
Gross Profit	0.625
Gross Profit %	1.15%
Holding Period (expect a 07/01/97 payment)	27 days
Annualized Rate of Return	15.53%

Example 131 (7/97)

Nellcor Puritan Bennett Inc. (NELL - $28 1/4 - OTC) signed a definitive agreement to be acquired by Mallinckrodt Inc. (MKG-$35-NYSE) for $1.9 billion in cash, combining the medical products companies, in a bid to expand MKG's core medical products business. MKG has begun a $28.50 per share cash tender offer to acquire all of NELL's 63 million outstanding shares. St. Louis-based MKG's hospital products include X-ray contrast media, radiopharmaceuticals and devices for imaging. NELL, based in Pleasanton, California, provides medical products for the home and hospital that monitor, diagnose and treat patients with respiratory impairments. The offer is subject to a majority of NELL's shares being tendered in the offer as well as the receipt of all necessary regulatory approvals. The withdrawal and expiration of the tender offer is August 25, 1997. We have a position in NELL.

NELL	$28.500
Net Dividends & Short Interest	.000
Poison Pill Redemption	.000
Net Expected Proceeds	$28.500
Current	$28.250
Plus Transaction Costs	0.015
	$28.265
Gross Profit	0.235
Gross Profit %	0.83%
Holding Period (expect a 08/27/97 payment)	22 days
Annualized Rate of Return	13.8%

Example 132 (8/97)

American Medserve Corp. (AMCI - $17 13/16 - OTC) agreed to be acquired by Omnicare Inc. (OCR-$30 3/8-NYSE) for $234 million in cash, extending OCR's pharmacy services to six new states and expanding them in five others. OCR has begun an $18 per share cash tender offer for all of AMCI's outstanding shares. The purchase is OCR's seventh since April, as the company builds a network of pharmacies serving nursing homes, retirement centers and other long-term care facilities. AMCI adds sites in Colorado, Louisiana, Minnesota, Nebraska, Maryland and South Dakota to that network. After the transaction OCR will serve about 413,000 patients at 5,100 sites in 35 states. AMCI manages pharmacy services for about 51,400 residents in 720 facilities in 11 states. The transaction has received all necessary approvals. The withdrawal and expiration of the tender offer is September 11, 1997. We have established a position in AMCI.

AMCI	$18.000
Net Dividends & Short Interest	.000
Poison Pill Redemption	.000
Net Expected Proceeds	$18.000
Current	$17.813
Plus Transaction Costs	0.015
	$17.828
Gross Profit	0.172
Gross Profit %	0.96%
Holding Period (expect a 09/16/97 payment)	12 days
Annualized Rate of Return	29.3%

Example 133 (9/97)

Tejas Gas Corp. (TEJ - $59 7/8 - NYSE) signed a definitive agreement to be acquired by The Royal Dutch Shell Group's U.S. arm for $2.35 billion in cash and debt, giving Shell Oil the pipelines it needs to transport natural gas production from the Gulf of Mexico. Shell Oil, the U.S. unit, will pay $61.50 per share in cash, or $1.45 billion. Shell will also assume about $900 million in debt and preferred stock. TEJ has 10,500 miles of natural gas pipelines, including extensive networks in Texas and Louisiana that Shell will link with its Gulf pipelines. Many companies in the natural gas industry have been sold in the last two years, bought largely by utilities who want to sell both natural gas and electricity and secure sources of fuel for power generation. In addition to its pipelines, TEJ owns underground storage facilities that can hold 155 billion cubic feet of natural gas and 14 processing plants used to separate liquid fuels such as propane and butane from natural gas before it is shipped. The merger is subject to shareholder and regulatory approval and is expected to be completed by year-end. We have a position in TEJ.

TEJ	$61.500
Net Dividends & Short Interest	.000
Poison Pill Redemption	.000
Net Expected Proceeds	61.500
Current	$59.875
Plus Transaction Costs	0.025
	59.890
Gross Profit	1.625
Gross Profit %	2.71%
Holding Period (expect a 12/15/97 payment)	70 days
Annualized Rate of Return	14.15%

Example 134 (10/97)

Greenfield Industries Inc. (GFII - $37 3/4 - OTC) agreed to be acquired by Kennametal Inc. (KMT-$48 1/2-NYSE) through a $38 per share cash tender offer, adding the No.1 drill-bit maker to KMT's line of industrial metalworking tools. The acquisition gives KMT a toehold in the consumer market. GFII, which had 1996 sales of $520 million and earnings of $26.2 million, has been the exclusive supplier of Craftsman drill bits to Sears since 1930. The transaction has received U.S. antitrust approval but still requires German antitrust clearance. The withdrawal and expiration of the tender offer is November 14, 1997. We have established a position in GFII.

GFII	$38.000
Net Dividends & Short Interest	.000
Poison Pill Redemption	.000
Net Expected Proceeds	$38.000
Current	$37.750
Plus Transaction Costs	0.020
	37.770
Gross Profit	0.230
Gross Profit %	0.61%
Holding Period (expect a 11/19/97 payment)	14 days
Annualized Rate of Return	15.88%

Example 135 (11/97)

Amati Communications Corporation (AMTX - $19 3/4 - OTC) agreed to be acquired by Texas Instruments Inc. (TXN-$49 5/8-NYSE) in an all-cash tender offer valued at $20 per share, or $395 million. Amati, a San Jose-based company, has a digital modem technology, known as Digital Subscriber Line (DSL), that allows ordinary telephone lines to carry audio, video and data information about 200 times faster than today's typical modems. The bid surpasses a $394 million all-stock offer from Westell Technologies Inc. (WSTL-$16 5/8-OTC) to issue 0.9 of its shares for each of Amati's 19.7 million common shares. To break that agreement, Amati must pay Westell a $14.8 million fee. In addition, TXN also entered into an alliance with Westell to incorporate TXN's and AMTX's technology into Westell's modem systems. TXN commenced the all-cash tender offer on November 25, 1997 and it is scheduled to expire on December 23, 1997. We have established a position in AMTX.

AMTX	$20.000
Net Dividends & Short Interest	.000
Poison Pill Redemption	.000
Net Expected Proceeds	$20.000
Current	$19.750
Plus Transaction Costs	0.015
	$19.765
Gross Profit	0.235
Gross Profit %	1.19%
Holding Period (expect a 12/29/97 payment)	26 days
Annualized Rate of Return	16.69%

Example 136 (12/97)

Spine-Tech, Inc. (SPYN - $51 1/2 - OTC) agreed to be acquired by Sulzer Medica Ltd. (SM-$23 1/4-NYSE), a leading cardiovascular and orthopedic implant company headquartered in Switzerland, for $595 million in cash. The transaction involves a cash tender offer by SM for all the outstanding SPYN common shares at $52 per share. Spine-Tech is one of a handful of companies pioneering a minimally invasive surgical implant to treat degenerative disorders of the spine. The implants are placed in the spine opening created after a damaged disc is removed to help the vertebrae move together. The company's leading product is the BAK Interbody Fusion System, an innovative system of spinal implants and instruments which are used to promote spinal fusion in patients suffering from chronic, disabling back pain resulting from degenerative disc disease. In October, SPYN won FDA approval to sell a second-generation spine implant that can be used for smaller patients, while main rival Sofamor Danek failed to win the backing of an FDA panel for a competing device. SPYN can now continue to sell their devices for up to 12 months with no other competition. The expiration of the tender offer is January 20, 1998. We have established a position in SPYN.

SPYN	$52.000
Net Dividends & Short Interest	.000
Poison Pill Redemption	.000
Net Expected Proceeds	$52.000
Current	$51.500
Plus Transaction Costs	0.015
	$51.515
Gross Profit	0.485
Gross Profit %	0.94%
Holding Period (expect a 1/23/98 payment)	17 days
Annualized Rate of Return	20.21%

Example 137 (1/98)

Trident International, Inc. (TRDT - $16 3/8 - OTC), a maker of ink-jet technology, agreed to be acquired by Illinois Tool Works Inc. (ITW-$60 3/8-NYSE) through a $16.50 per share cash tender offer. ITW will gain TRDT's patented impulse ink-jet printheads, which are used for printing information such as bar codes and addresses on shipping containers. ITW already has ink-jet printing capabilities, although its system can't be used for bar codes. TRDT plans to continue selling its product to other companies after the sale. Carton coding -- putting information on shipping containers -- accounts for about 70 percent of TRDT's business. TRDT's products are also used for canceling checks at high speeds, addressing mail and canceling postal stamps. The transaction has received all necessary regulatory approvals and is only conditioned on ITW obtaining a majority of TRDT's shares in the tender offer. The withdrawal and expiration of the tender offer is Feb. 10. We have established a position in TRDT.

TRDT	$16.500
Net Dividends & Short Interest	.000
Poison Pill Redemption	.000
	$16.500
Current	$16.375
Plus Transaction Costs	.025
	$16.400
Gross Profit	$0.10
Gross Profit %	0.61%
Holding Period (expect a 2/15/99 payment)	15 days
Annualized Rate of Return	14.83%

Example 138 (2/98)

Wonderware Corporation (WNDR - $23 5/8 - OTC) entered into a definitive agreement to be acquired by Siebe Plc (SIBEY-$42 1/2-OTC) for $24 per share in cash, or approximately $375 million. Siebe Plc, based in Windsor, Berkshire, is one of Britain's largest diversified engineering and electronics groups, incorporating more than 200 companies and employing more than 50,000 people worldwide. Siebe Plc has initiated a cash tender offer for all outstanding shares for WNDR to complete the transaction, which is expected to occur in April of 1998. The offer is subject to the condition that a majority of the shares are tendered and other customary conditions. Siebe expects to finance the acquisition of WNDR with its existing lines of credit. Founded in 1987, WNDR pioneered Microsoft Windows-based software for developing industrial automation applications. The company's FactorySuite software product line is an integrated suite of easy-to-use software tools for creating factory applications that helps companies like Coca-Cola Co. control and monitor factory processes. The acquisition will give WNDR access to a worldwide sales and distribution network, and Siebe will be able to market the products with its process-control system as a complete package. We have a position in WNDR

WNDR	$24.000
Net Dividends & Short Interest	.000
Poison Pill Redemption	.000
Net Expected Proceeds	$24.000
Current	$23.625
Plus Transaction Costs	0.015
	$23.640
Gross Profit	0.36
Gross Profit %	1.52%
Holding Period (expect a 04/06/98 payment)	33 days
Annualized Rate of Return	16.84%

Example 139 (3/98)

Ticketmaster Group, Inc. (TKTM - $29 1/2 - OTC) accepted a sweetened bid from USA Networks, Inc. (USAI-$27 -OTC) for about $400 million, or $29.70 a share, in stock. Following protests by Ticketmaster executives and investors that the first offer was too low, USAI boosted its bid by 17 percent. In October, USAI offered about $340 million, or $25.30, in an unsolicited bid for the half of Ticketmaster that USA Networks doesn't own. Under the new agreement, USA Networks will swap 1.126 share for each Ticketmaster share, up from 1.012 share. USAI, which was then known as HSN, Inc., bought the first half of TKTM from its chairman, Paul Allen, for $235.8 million. USAI wants to use TKTM, the nation's largest seller of tickets to events such as concerts, to boost its expansion into on-line shopping. USAI also owns Home Shopping Network, the television retailer whose large telephone ordering system will complement TKTM's. The transaction is expected to be completed by the end of June. We continue to hold a position in TKTM.

TKTM (1 TKTM=1.126 USAI)	$30.402
Net Dividends & Short Interest	.310
Poison Pill Redemption	.000
Net Expected Proceeds	$30.712
Current	$29.500
Plus Transaction Costs	0.030
	$29.530
Gross Profit	1.182
Gross Profit %	4.00%
Holding Period (expect 06/30/98 close)	90 days
Annualized Rate of Return	16.23%

Example 140 (4/98)

Simulation Sciences Inc. (SMCI - $9 3/4 - OTC) agreed to be acquired by Siebe Plc (SEBE-Bp 1336-FTSE), the U.K. electronic equipment maker, through a $10 per share cash tender offer. SMCI's software helps petroleum and petrochemical companies optimize production and manage information. The acquisition comes less than two months after SEBE agreed to pay $375 million for Wonderware Corp., which sells software that controls and monitors factory processes. Both Wonderware's and SMCI's products run on Microsoft's Windows operating system. SMCI is a recognized global leader in process organization and simulation software, and this acquisition will allow SEBE to significantly extend its presence into the rapidly growing $650 million process simulation and modeling market. The acquisition broadens SEBE's software line, which includes systems that manage factories and buildings. SMCI will benefit from a more extensive distribution system and greater levels of service. The transaction has received all necessary regulatory approvals and is set to expire on May 18, 1998. We have a position in SMCI.

SMCI	$10.000
Net Dividends & Short Interest	.000
Poison Pill Redemption	.000
Net Expected Proceeds	$10.000
Current	$ 9.750
Plus Transaction Costs	0.015
	$ 9.765
Gross Profit	0.235
Gross Profit %	2.41%
Holding Period (expect a 05/21/98 close)	21 days
Annualized Rate of Return	41.8%

Example 141 (5/98)

Donnelley Enterprise Solutions Inc. (DEZI - $20 5/8 - OTC) agreed to be acquired by Bowne & Co., Inc. (BNE-$43 1/8-NYSE), the world's largest financial printer, through a $21 per share cash tender offer. R.R. Donnelley & Sons Co., a commercial printer that owns 2.1 million DEZI shares, or approximately 43%, has agreed to tender its shares into the offer. BNE is the global market leader in the field of empowering information by combining superior customer service with appropriate new technologies to manage and distribute a client's information to any audience, through any medium, in any language, anywhere in the world. DEZI is a single-service provider of integrated information management solutions to professional service organizations, primarily large law firms, investment banks and accounting firms. The addition of DEZI will substantially increase BNE's existing outsourcing solution offerings. The withdrawal and expiration of the tender offer is July 1, 1998. We have established a position in DEZI.

DEZI	$21.000
Net Dividends & Short Interest	.000
Poison Pill Redemption	.000
Net Expected Proceeds	$21.000
Current	$20.625
Plus Transaction Costs	0.015
	$20.640
Gross Profit	0.360
Gross Profit %	1.74%
Holding Period (expect a 07/06/98 close)	36 days
Annualized Rate of Return	17.6%

Example 142 (6/98)

Triangle Pacific Corporation (TRIP - $55 - OTC) agreed to be acquired by Armstrong World Industries, Inc. (ACK-$67 3/8-NYSE), a floor coverings company, for $1.15 billion in cash and assumed debt. ACK will pay $890 million in cash, or $55.50 a share, to TRIP shareholders. Dallas-based TRIP makes hardwood flooring products and kitchen and bathroom cabinets. ACK, the top North American maker of vinyl floor coverings, is hoping to expand its presence in other areas of the hard-floor covering market. Once ACK finishes buying TRIP, it will be the second largest maker of floor coverings in the world after Shaw Industries Inc., a carpet maker, and the largest maker of hard-floor coverings in the world. The expiration of the tender offer is July 17. We have a position in TRIP.

TRIP	$55.500
Net Dividends & Short Interest	.000
Poison Pill Redemption	.000
Net Expected Proceeds	$55.500
Current	$55.000
Plus Transaction Costs	0.015
	$55.015
Gross Profit	0.485
Gross Profit %	0.88%
Holding Period (expect a 7/21/98 close)	21 days
Annualized Rate of Return	15.32%

Example 143 (7/98)

BetzDearborn, Inc. (BTL - $67 1/8 - NYSE) agreed to be bought by Hercules, Inc. (HPC-$34 3/4-NYSE), a U.S. specialty chemicals maker, for $3.1 billion in cash and assumed debt, creating one of the world's biggest makers of chemicals used in paper-making, water-treatment and other industrial processes. HPC, which had $1.87 billion in 1997 sales, is offering $72 per BTL share. It will also assume debt of $700 million. BTL is the No. 2 U.S. producer of water-treatment and industrial-process chemicals with $1.29 billion in 1997 sales. The purchase allows Wilmington, Delaware-based HPC, itself the subject of takeover speculation after it was outbid by Ciba Specialty Chemicals AG for the European chemical company Allied Colloids Plc earlier this year, to resume its worldwide expansion amid industry consolidation. It also gives HPC a complementary range of paper-processing and water treatment chemicals that it doesn't currently offer. HPC paper chemicals are used primarily to improve strength and other paper qualities. BTL's chemicals are used to protect equipment and increase efficiency in paper manufacturing. The transaction, which is subject to approval by BTL shareholders, is expected to close in the fourth quarter. We have established a position in BTL.

BTL	$72.000
Net Dividends & Short Interest	.000
Poison Pill Redemption	.000
Net Expected Proceeds	$72.000
Current	$67.125
Plus Transaction Costs	.015
	$67.140
Gross Profit	4.860
Gross Profit %	7.24%
Holding Period (expect 11/30/98)	122 days
Annualized Rate of Return	21.66%

Example 144 (8/98)

Dravo Corporation (DRV - $12 5/8 - NYSE) agreed to be bought by Belgium's Carmeuse SA for $191.3 million. Closely held Carmeuse plans to roll DRV, the largest publicly held U.S. producer of lime used in cement, into a pending joint venture with France's Lafarge S.A. Carmeuse has begun a tender offer at $13 per share for all of DRV's 14.7 million shares outstanding. Completion of the transaction depends on DRV stockholders tendering at least half of the shares and the receipt of regulatory approvals. The agreement provides for a breakup fee of $9.5 million should Pittsburgh-based DRV accept a higher bid from a third party. The transaction isn't subject to completion of the previously announced line joint venture between Carmeuse and Lafarge, a leading maker of cement and concrete. After the transaction is completed in the fourth quarter, the DRV business will become part of the venture, which will make Lafarge an international player in lime. The withdrawal and expiration of the tender offer is October 19, 1998. We have established a position in DRV.

DRV	$13.000
Net Dividends & Short Interest	.000
Poison Pill Redemption	.000
Net Expected Proceeds	$13.000
Current	$12.625
Plus Transaction Costs	.025
	$12.650
Gross Profit	0.35
Gross Profit %	2.77%
Holding Period (expect a 10/21/98 return)	16 days
Annualized Rate of Return	63.18%

Example 145 (10/98)

Mecklermedia Corporation (MECK - $28 7/16 - OTC) agreed to be acquired by Penton Media, Inc. (PME-$15-NYSE) for about $274 million in cash, or $29 per share. PME plans to take advantage of MECK's presence in Internet trade shows and conferences. MECK publishes the weekly magazine Internet World and a monthly magazine, Boardwatch. It also produces Internet trade shows and conferences. PME, spun off from Pittway Corp. in August, publishes magazines and CD-ROMs, and creates Web sites. It plans to combine its products with MECK's Internet operations. The acquisition fits in with PME's previously announced plan to increase revenue through adding trade shows and conferences, which presents its biggest opportunity for new product growth.   PME said the acquisition will be financed primarily through additional borrowings. DLJ, PME's financial advisor, will provide the financing for PME's tender offer and the acquisition, refinance existing PME debt, and pay related expenses. Alan Meckler, chairman and CEO of Westport, Connecticut-based MECK, will tender his stake in the company, which is about 30 percent. He also gave PME the option to buy his shares in case a third party tries to buy MECK. Both companies' boards have approved the acquisition. The tender offer expires on Nov. 18. We have a small position in MECK.

MECK	$29.0000
Net Dividends & Short Interest	.0000
Poison Pill Redemption	.0000
Net Expected Proceeds	$29.0000
Current	$28.4375
Plus Transaction Costs	.0250
	$28.4625
Gross Profit	0.5375
Gross Profit %	1.89%
Holding Period (expect a 11/25/98 return)	23 days
Annualized Rate of Return	29.97%

Example 146 (11/98)

CN Biosciences, Inc. (CNBI - $24 1/2 - OTC) agreed to be bought by Merck KGaA (MRX-DEM 69-Frankfurt), Germany's fifth-largest drugs and chemicals maker, for about $150 million. MRX, which makes the world's best-selling non-insulin diabetes drug, Glucophage, offered $25 per share for CNBI. CNBI makes reagents, substances used in genetic-engineering research. MRX is also in talks with several U.S. companies about further acquisitions as it tries to expand in the world's biggest and fastest-growing pharmaceuticals market, adding it may reach a decision in January. The $244 billion global drugs market is expected to consolidate further. MRX is increasing the size of their distribution network in reagents and taking part in the microbiology revolution. MRX said the acquisition of CNBI, which will be part of MRX's laboratory-supplies division, signifies a decisive improvement of its market position in the fast-growing segment of bioreagents. San Diego, California-based MRX is expected to double its sales in five years. The tender offer expires on December 23. We have established a position in CNBI.

CNBI	$25.000
Net Dividends & Short Interest	.000
Poison Pill Redemption	.000
	$25.000
Current	$24.500
Plus Transaction Costs	.025
	24.525
Gross Profit	0.475
Gross Profit %	1.94%
Holding Period (expect 12/28/98)	28 days
Annualized Rate of Return	25.25%

Example 147 (12/98)

LCS Industries, Inc. (LCSI - $17 3/16 - OTC) agreed to be bought by Onex Corporation's (OCX-C$ 43.50-Toronto) CustomerOne Holding Corp. through a $17.50 cash tender offer, expanding OCX's outsourcing services for direct marketers. LCSI provides catalog-order fulfillment and other services for direct-marketing companies. OCX, a Toronto merchant bank with 1997 revenue of $11.2 billion, also has investments in steel-component making, construction and food services. The acquisition will expand the business of CustomerOne, a holding company for Softbank Services Group and North Direct Response. OCX acquired the two companies earlier this year to provide outsourcing services to Internet and computer companies and consumer package groups. It is a new platform OCX is developing through acquisitions of other companies and organic growth. The withdrawal and expiration of the tender offer is January 22, 1999. We have established a position in LCSI.

LCSI	$17.5000
Net Dividends & Short Interest	.0000
Poison Pill Redemption	.0000
	$17.5000
Current	$17.1875
Plus Transaction Costs	.0250
	$17.2125
Gross Profit	0.2875
Gross Profit %	1.67%
Holding Period (expect 1/27/99)	27 days
Annualized Rate of Return	22.58%

Example 148 (1/99)

Aeroquip-Vickers, Inc. (ANV - $56 5/8 - NYSE) agreed to be bought by Eaton Corporation (ETN-$69 3/8-NYSE) for about $1.7 billion in cash. ANV shareholders will receive $58 per share in a cash merger. ETN will rank behind Parker-Hannifin Corp. as a maker of hydraulics used for farm machinery, construction equipment and other industries. ANV's devices to control machines -- hydraulic pumps, electric motors and electronic controls -- will give ETN a range of products to serve industrial customers who seek diversity form vendors. Hydraulic equipment places liquids such as water, oil or specialty chemicals under pressure to control the motion of machinery. ANV and ETN share a number of major customers, including Boeing Co., Ford Motor Co. and Deere & Co. The hydraulics industry, which worldwide is valued at $30 billion, is made up of many small companies, and ETN and Parker-Hannifin are expected to make a number of smaller acquisitions. This transaction gives ETN the muscle to remain competitive during the industry's consolidation. We expect the merger to close on April 8. We have established a position in ETN.

ANV	$58.000
Net Dividends & Short Interest	.000
Poison Pill Redemption	.000
	$58.000
Current	$56.625
Plus Transaction Costs	.025
	$56.650
Gross Profit	1.35
Gross Profit %	2.38%
Holding Period (expect 4/13/99)	42 days
Annualized Rate of Return	20.71%

Example 149 (3/99)

United States Filter Corporation (USF - $30 5/8 - NYSE) agreed to be bought by Vivendi SA (EX-Euro 227.9-Paris), France's biggest water utility, for about $7.9 billion in cash and assumed debt, to help EX gain a bigger share of the global water-treatment market. EX is offering $31.50 for each share of USF and would assume $1.7 billion in debt. The purchase will make EX's water business the world's largest and help it outbid rivals for water-treatment contracts by cutting its equipment costs. USF, owner of Culligan Water Technologies, has high sales and brand recognition in the U.S., but has trouble winning contracts for water-treatment projects elsewhere because it lacked EX's reputation and size. EX, with revenue of about $35 billion, is a world leader in construction, public works, telecommunications and civil engineering as well as water supply. USF will add $4.9 billion to EX's annual sales. The sale is a turnabout for USF, which bought more than 160 companies since its creation in 1990 but stumbled when it doubled long-term debt by buying Culligan in July. EX's water unit will have $12 billion in annual sales, making it the market leader in a business expected to grow rapidly. EX intends to sell shares worth 3 billion euros ($3.26 billion) and convertible bonds worth 2 billion euros to pay for the transaction. For EX, USF will help the French company regain ground lost in the U.S. market in the past year to its French rival, Suez Lyonnaise des Eaux SA. The expiration of the tender offer is April 22, 1999. We have established a large position in USF.

USF	$31.500
Net Dividends & Short Interest	.000
Poison Pill Redemption	.000
	$31.500
Current	$30.625
Plus Transaction Costs	.025
	$30.650
Gross Profit	0.85
Gross Profit %	2.77%
Holding Period (expect 4/30/99)	24 days
Annualized Rate of Return	42.13%

Example 150 (4/99)

FORE Systems, Inc. (FORE - $33 3/4 - OTC) agreed to be bought by General Electric Company plc (GEC-GBp 658.5 - London), Britain's largest electrical engineering company, for $4.5 billion in cash, extending GEC's push into the fast-growing U.S. market for communications equipment. FORE makes advanced computer-networking switches used by phone companies to combine data with regular phone traffic. GEC will pay $35 per share. GEC is shedding its defense business to focus on networking equipment, kicking off the strategy in March with the $2.1 billion purchase of U.S.-based Reltec Corp. GEC's purchases of Reltec and Fore come as other European equipment companies expand their product lines. The tender offer is scheduled to expire on May 20, 1999. In order to receive all regulatory approvals, we expect it to be extended to mid-to-late June. We have established a position in FORE.

FORE	$35.000
Net Dividends & Short Interest	.000
Poison Pill Redemption	.000
	$35.000
Current	$33.750
Plus Transaction Costs	.025
	$33.775
Gross Profit	1.225
Gross Profit %	3.63%
Holding Period (expect 6/24/99)	55 days
Annualized Rate of Return	24.07%

Example 151 (5/99)

Daniel Industries, Inc. (DAN - $21 - NYSE) agreed to be acquired by Emerson Electric Co. (EMR- $67 1/8-NYSE) for $460 million in cash and assumed debt, expanding EMR's line of metering equipment. EMR, the world's largest electric-motor maker, said it would pay $21.25 in cash for each share of DAN, a maker of meters for oil and natural gas pipelines. EMR will use DAN's product line to expand sales of meters and other monitoring equipment to the oil industry, utilities, paper manufacturers and other large industrial users. In March, DAN turned down a $292 million buyout offer from an unidentified company, and hired Simmons & Co. International to review its options. About 63 percent of DAN's energy-related revenue comes from natural gas, and EMR believes its purchase would particularly strengthen its offerings in the natural-gas industry. The expiration of the tender offer is June 8, 1999. We have established a position in DAN.

DAN	$21.250
Net Dividends & Short Interest	.000
Poison Pill Redemption	.000
	$21.250
Current	$21.000
Plus Transaction Costs	.025
	$21.025
Gross Profit	0.225
Gross Profit %	1.07%
Holding Period (expect 6/17/99)	15 days
Annualized Rate of Return	26.04%

Example 152 (6/99)

Rental Service Corp. (RSV - $28 5/8 - NYSE), the No.3 U.S. equipment-rental company, agreed to be purchased by Atlas Copco AB (ATCOA-SEK231.5-Stockholm), a Swedish manufacturer of compressors and electric tools, for $1.63 billion, or $29 per share in cash. ATCOA's offer tops a previous bid of $22.75 from United Rentals, the No. 1 U.S. equipment rental company, that had been rejected by RSV as inadequate. The RSV-ATCOA transaction would create the second largest equipment-rental company in North America, with annual sales of $1.2 billion. The equipment rental industry has grown at an annual rate of 20 percent in the past few years as strong U.S. construction spending has fueled equipment rentals by firms like Dow Chemical and Bayer AG. But the industry remains fragmented with about 12,000 companies operating in North America.

RSV	$29.000
Net Dividends & Short Interest	.000
Poison Pill Redemption	.000
	$29.000
Current	$28.625
Plus Transaction Costs	.020
	$28.645
Gross Profit	0.355
Gross Profit %	1.24%
Holding Period (expect 7/30/99)	25 days
Annualized Rate of Return	18.09%

Endnotes

[1] Smith, Roy C. *The Money Wars: the Rise and Fall of the Great Buyout Boom of the 1980s,* New York, 1990, pp. 60-61.

[2] *The Money Wars,* pp. 141-142.

[3] Wasserstein, Bruce. *Big Deal,* New York, 1998, p. 124.

[4] Boesky, Ivan F. *Merger Mania,* New York, 1985, p. 15.

[5] "The Future of Risk Arbitrage," *Investment Dealers' Digest,* April 23, 1990, p. 17.

[6] "Risk Arbitrage for the Mind," *Business Week,* May 29, 1995, p.82.

[7] 14D-9 merger document, Neutrogena Corporation / Johnson & Johnson, August 26, 1994, p.7.

[8] 14D-1 merger document, Goulds Pumps, Inc. / ITT Industries, Inc., April 25, 1997, p. 14.

[9] Section 7 of the Clayton Antitrust Act of 1914, as amended by the Celler-Kefauver Act of 1950.

[10] Takeover Teardrop: Arbs Lose Amid Merger Boom," *The Wall Street Journal,* February 27, 1996, p. C1.

[11] "A New Breed of Wolf At the Corporate Door," *The New York Times,* March 19, 1997, p. D1.

Index

Ren Corp., 165

Rental Service Corp., 185

Revco, 145

RHI Entertainment, 158

Rhone-Poulenc Rorer, 57-58

Rhone-Poulenc SA, 57-58

RJR Nabisco, 14, 23, 123

Rorer Group Inc., 131

Ryan Homes, 112

S

Safeway, 109

Salem Carpet Mill, Inc., 146

Sanford Corp., 145

Schaefer Value Trust, 133

Scott & Fetzer, 103

Sheller-Globe, 107

Simulation Sciences Inc., 179

Skadden, Arps, 69

SmithKline Beecham Plc, 76-77

Southland Corp., 116

Sperry Corp., 108

Spine-Tech, Inc., 177

Square D Company, 138

Standard Oil, 13, 15

Staples Inc., 38-39

Starwood Lodging , 89-90

Storer Communications, 104

Syratech Corp., 61-62

T

Taft Broadcasting, 115

Tambrands, 52-53

Tejas Gas Corp., 175

Telecom USA, 132

Tellabs, 27

Texas Eastern Corp., 124

Thrifty Rent-a-Car, 126

Ticketmaster Group, Inc., 178

Tivoli Systems Inc., 167

Tony Lama Inc., 137

TPC Corp., 173

Triangle Pacific Corporation, 180

Triconex Corp., 161

Trident International, Inc., 177

Tyco International Ltd., 26

Tylan General, 172

U

Union Carbide Consumer Division Rights, 108

Union Pacific Resources, 85-86

United Airlines, 24-25

United Artists Entertainment, 140

United Energy Resources, 105

United States Filter Corporation, 183

US West NewVector Group Inc., 139

USG Corp., 119

V

VeloBind, Inc., 136

Viacom International, 111

Vista Chemical Co., 138

W

Wachtell, Lipton, 69

Warner Communications, 127

Wonderware Corporation, 178